ANDERSONVILLE
CIVIL WAR
PRISON

ANDERSONVILLE CIVIL WAR PRISON

ROBERT SCOTT DAVIS

Charleston — London

THE
History
PRESS

Published by The History Press
Charleston, SC 29403
www.historypress.net

Cover image: Prisoner Thomas O'Dea's rendering of the Andersonville prison. *Courtesy of the Library of Congress.*

First published 2010

Manufactured in the United States

ISBN 978.1.59629.762.3

Davis, Robert Scott, 1954-
Andersonville Civil War Prison / Robert Scott Davis.
p. cm.
Includes bibliographical references and index.
ISBN 978-1-59629-762-3
1. Andersonville Prison--History. 2. Andersonville Prison--History--Pictorial works. 3. Prisoners of war--Georgia--Andersonville--History--19th century. 4. Prisoners of war--Confederate States of America--History. 5. Prisoners of war--United States--History--19th century. 6. United States--History--Civil War, 1861-1865--Prisoners and prisons. 7. United States--History--Civil War, 1861-1865--Atrocities. I. Title.
E612.A5D152 2010
973.7'71--dc22
2010040672

In memory of Jack Lundquist (died September 16, 2009),
a diligent researcher and a good friend.

CONTENTS

INTRODUCTION

Andersonville was the popular name given to the Confederate Civil War prison Camp Sumter in then Sumter County (today's Macon County), Georgia, by the prison's personnel and prisoners. This installation operated from late February 1864 to early May 1865 and held some forty thousand different civilians, white officers of African American soldiers and enlisted soldiers and sailors of all races. Officers of white Federal units were held at special prisons such as Camp Oglethorpe in Macon, Georgia, and Libby Prison in Richmond, Virginia. The some thirteen thousand men buried in the prison's cemetery and the thousands more who subsequently died from having been imprisoned there became such legends that they inspired a bestselling history by a prisoner, a Pulitzer Prize–winning novel and an Emmy Award–winning play. Andersonville has been the subject of more books than any other prison in the world. Built by slaves who later often helped prisoners escape, this prison also has a secret African American history represented by one of Winslow Homer's most important paintings. Today, millions of people have family connections to America's deadliest place of incarceration.

The notoriety of Andersonville, however, has also created other legends, from simple misunderstandings to gross partisan distortions of the facts. Even during the Civil War, many Americans mistakenly thought that it was the only Confederate, or even the only Civil War, prison. More than 150 other places were used as prisons during the Civil War (1861–1865), including, for holding Federal civilians, Castle Thunder and, for captured Union enlisted men, Belle Island, both in Richmond, Virginia.

The two greatest and most misleading myths of Andersonville (Camp Sumter) began during the war, partially as propaganda: that it served as some sort of extermination facility for captured United States soldiers and sailors and that prisons in the North were equally as bad. About one out of three of the men who entered the gates of Camp Sumter remain there today in the national cemetery, having died from malnutrition, exposure, disease and, in a few instances, violence at the hands of other prisoners and the guards. Thousands of other prisoners died from the effects of time in this open-air stockade after transfer to other prisons or release. Many of the camp's former inmates never fully recovered physically, mentally or emotionally from their experiences.

No one deliberately conspired to murder the inmates of Andersonville, although initially few white Southerners offered any sympathy either. Confederate bureaucrats, frightened by wartime security and local political sensibilities, unintentionally chose an isolated site for the prison that lacked the resources to produce or import adequate supplies for the prison built there. The failures of incompetent administrators also resulted in the starvation of the Confederate population. Civilians, however, could find refuge, even behind Federal lines, and soldiers were free to forage (steal) from farms they encountered. Incompetence existed in the North too, but without invasion and a national siege, the United States' wartime economy expanded its considerable agricultural and industrial resources, as well as its efficient railroad system.

Abundance covered many failures, although many civilians and soldiers did suffer in the wartime North; other citizens grew rich off the war, as in the much more under-resourced South. Brigadier General John H. Winder, commandant of Andersonville and commander of the Confederate prisons east of the Mississippi River, finally called for the Confederacy to release the prisoners. After he directed the construction of the much more suitable prison at Millen, Georgia, he had the population at Andersonville reduced by transfers to a supportable population that eventually would have barracks and a hospital building. Even inspectors who condemned the prison during the worst months still complimented Captain Henry Wirz, Winder's subordinate, for his efficiency. Many of the prisoners would speak out in the captain's defense during and after the trial of Wirz for war crimes by a United States military commission after the war.

Similarly, as Southerners lost family members during the war and the eventual outcome of their struggles and sacrifices became obvious, many of them felt that the Northern invaders deserved whatever terrible fate they

John H. Winder. *Courtesy of the Library of Congress.*

found in the South. They also wanted to believe that Confederate soldiers were deliberately mistreated and starved in the far more prosperous North. Pamphlets making those arguments, including accounts by exchanged or escaped prisoners, appeared in the South even before the war ended. This anger evolved into arguments that joined the excuses for slavery and the Civil War that continue to be made today.

No prison, North or South, deserved to be compared to Andersonville and its official prisoner mortality rate of 28.12 percent, or from a more credible 31.58 percent to as high as 35 percent. By contrast, in both armies, deaths reached 12 to 15 percent, close to the same percentage for men who died in captivity. Some officials at Federal prisons such as Camp Douglas could have done more for their charges, but the worst United States installation, Elmira, had a mortality rate of only 24 percent, and that due in part to a brutal northern winter. Confederate prisons in Salisbury, North Carolina, and Florence, South Carolina, reached a scale of death that approached that of Andersonville, but mercifully, they were not open long enough to create an equal tragedy. Some sources credit Salisbury with a possibly higher mortality rate—34 percent—than Andersonville. More likely, Salisbury came in at only 25 percent overall, but whatever its death rate, it counts among its burials men who actually died as a result of their time at Andersonville. One veteran estimated that by 1890, only some eight or nine hundred of the almost forty thousand Andersonville inmates still lived.

This page and next: Prison survivors and persons pretending to have been at Andersonville went on speaking tours, published memoirs and prepared prints of the infamous prison camp. The illustrations, ranging from simplistic to grandiose, were usually inaccurate, as shown by these examples. *Courtesy of the Library of Congress; the Hargrett Rare Book and Manuscripts Library, University of Georgia Libraries.*

The final great myths of Andersonville involve the failure to end this humanitarian catastrophe. Throughout history, no nation readily gave up its enemy captives, and the Confederate States of America proved to be no different. General William Tecumseh Sherman conducted a successful campaign across Georgia that did little physical damage but became one of the most successful uses of terrorism in military history. He avoided fighting battles, encouraging guerillas, destroying private property, inspiring slave escapes or rescuing prisoners in his effort to hurry the end of the war with as much a race as a march to the sea. His cavalry corps, however, largely found themselves inmates at Andersonville after a failed effort to release the prisoners. Most of the men they had sought to save had been moved to Camp Millen, Georgia, and other prisons, always beyond Sherman's efforts to rescue them. Selected words from an 1865 letter from General Grant to President Lincoln explaining how releasing Confederate prisoners would have cruelly extended the war omits that he had also ordered an exchange of Rebel soldiers who wanted to leave the Federal prison camps. Bureaucratic incompetence in both armies delayed the final release of the men held by both sides until the war ended.

Today, Andersonville National Historic Site has a national cemetery and a museum dedicated to the experiences of all American prisoners of war in all wars. The original prison's forts and some of its stockade have been restored. The park headquarters has an archive and an online database of the prisoners, guards and other Civil War personnel connected with the site's Civil War history. For information on visiting the park, see its website: http://www.nps.gov/ande/index.htm.

1

PRISONS OF WAR

Recent compilations of names of Civil War soldiers suggest that the ratio of the total number of men who served in some form or fashion in the Confederate military to the total number who served, at least some time, in the Federal forces may only come to 2:3. Incomplete records, service in different units, bounty deserters under false names, etc., cloud any definitive accounting, but it must be assumed that all of the South's soldiers combined could have held back their enemy indefinitely, at least on paper—a point made by Jefferson Davis in his speeches in the last days of his nation.

The reason the South lost its war of independence, however, had little to do with the sum total of available manpower; rather, it was directly related to how many men each side could support in the field on any day of the conflict. To arrive at these numbers, the researcher has to look at the interrelationships of civilian support, industrialization, transportation, finance, politics, use of military force, African American labor, education, strategy and much more. The United States in 1860 had no experience in nationwide bureaucracy and operations beyond running the post office. As two nations from 1861 to 1865, each of the competing federations of states had to learn how to manage its military and civilian resources. A solid and appropriate history of the Civil War could be written on how each succeeded and failed. In a narrower context, a study could also be made of how those problems were dealt with in relation to how each side dealt with its respective prisoners of war.

One of the least remembered horrors of Andersonville was how families learned that loved ones died under such terrible conditions. Some prisoners likely used false identities to shield family members from the knowledge of their fates. Former prisoner Thomas O'Dea inspired these drawings.

In earlier wars, the numbers of prisoners of war and the length of the war provided no special problems, but according to historian Lonnie R. Speer, during the American Civil War, by contrast, 674,000 men were taken captive, of whom some 410,000 were held in more than 150 detention facilities, from open ground to common jails to formal prison complexes. Only about 10 facilities on each side accounted for almost all of the deaths: 30,218 men died while held by the Confederacy (15 percent of the total number held), and 25,796 died while held by the United States (more than 12 percent of the number held).

The true hardships of the captives of the Civil War began with the breakdown of the prisoner exchange. From 1861 to 1863, the opposing sides largely dealt with the problem of prisoners by releasing the captured, by rank, through temporary internment camps on a fairly regular basis, but especially under the cartel of July 1862. During that time, the Confederacy operated Belle Island, Cahawba, Danville, Libby and Salisbury as principal holding areas. Following the huge defeats suffered by the Confederate armies in the Gettysburg, Vicksburg and Port Hudson campaigns in July 1863, the general exchange of prisoners broke down, although some local exchanges by individual commanders continued. By August 1864, Speer estimated that the Confederacy held 50,000 men, and the United States held another 67,500 inmates.

The Rebel armies wasted away from casualties, sickness, desertion, capture, surrender and draft evasion, with the Southern government having only a hope of replenishing its ranks from a prisoner exchange. Even that possibility diminished as continued Federal advances made it the better option for the North to wait out the war. A growing number of prisoners became an added burden to the Confederate States of America. The Southern nation had to build new prisons that were largely either open stockades or just open ground. Mortality figures for the prison camps, North and South, prove deceptive; even well-fed men died in the numerous epidemics that swept through any concentration of people (more men died in the Civil War armies from disease than from battle) due to the grossly inadequate medical knowledge of the time. No figures exist on men who died as a result of detention after they were released. Bureaucratic incompetence, corruption, revenge and politics in the North reduced rations for captured Confederates to the point that hungry Rebels ate rats.

In the worst of the Northern prisons, however, complaints were made over such problems as having wood instead of coal to burn in barrack stoves. By contrast, Union soldiers, sailors, and civilians held in such Southern camps as Camp Sumter (Andersonville) and Blackshear lived in holes in the ground, and they would have gladly traded places with their Northern counterparts at any time. In the Federal prison camps, incarcerated Rebels joined the Union military, became civilians who agreed to stay north of the Ohio River, or sometimes preferred even the worst Northern prison camp to returning to the degradation of the Southern armies. It is inconceivable that either government would have simply released the men it held when no other nation in history has ever done so.

In last months of 1863, the thousands of Federal prisoners being held indefinitely in Richmond, Virginia, became a threat to the Confederacy's very survival. The captives consumed precious rations at a time when the civilian residents of the Confederate capital were reduced to eating household pets to keep from starving. Hunger among the inmates of Richmond's Belle Island prison also drove the men there to capture and eat any dog. A mass escape from Belle Island and Libby Prisons could overwhelm the garrison of the Confederate capital and attack the civilian population. Richmond held half of the South's manufacturing and its only real cannon factories at a time when advancing Federal forces occupied much of Arkansas, Louisiana, Tennessee and Virginia, as well as many of the South's ports.

Desperate prisoners of war could thus have done damage to the Confederate States of America far beyond what Federal armies had achieved in two years of fighting on Virginia's battlefields. Union officers, as a group, did stage a mass escape from Libby Prison on February 9, 1864, and a Federal cavalry raid against Richmond, under Judson Kilpatrick, in that same month threatened to bring about a long-feared mass prisoner escape and, allegedly, even the assassination of President Jefferson Davis. Desertions from the Southern army and growing civilian opposition to the war, including food riots, by the civilians left the Confederate government increasingly unsure of whether its population would hinder or aid a mass prisoner escape.

Beyond resources and the progress of the war, neither side in the American Civil War found or even seemed to seriously seek moral high ground in its military prisons. Both warring nations, however, readily condemned the imaginary and the real policies of the other regarding prisoners of war. The Confederate government did not release men it could not afford to incarcerate after 1863, but the United States government could have also reopened the exchange of prisoners at little loss, and under almost any circumstances set by the collapsing Confederate government, on purely humanitarian grounds. Worse still, each side would excuse or commit atrocities based on reports—sometimes only rumors—of the sufferings of its own men in captivity. The Confederate States of America could also have eased the problems at Andersonville by continuing prisons at Cahawba and Belle Island with sustainable levels of capacity. That solution, however, would have been by a government operating with a competent bureaucracy and not by one overwhelmed by enemies and with hardly anything left but its deteriorating military and its prisoners. Later assassin John Wilkes Booth first planned to kidnap Abraham Lincoln to force the Federal government to resume the exchange of prisoners of war.

The solution for the South's security problem seemed to be to create a new prison or prisons far from the fighting, where local farms could supply the needs of guards and inmates. Brigadier General John H. Winder wanted to create a chain of incarceration facilities across the South, each small enough to be maintained by local resources and guarded by home guard–type local units. The panic resulting from the failed raid against Richmond in February 1864 replaced his practical solution with one unsustainable and overcrowded prison at an isolated railroad whistle-stop in an agricultural desert in deep southwest Georgia. Confederate officials rushed the prisoners of Belle Island and Cahawba to the new Camp Sumter (soon after popularly known as Andersonville) as the United States Army prepared for campaigns against Georgia and Virginia. Did that prison deserve its notorious reputation as America's great death camp? Has its infamy been overstated in contrast to Northern prisons? Who was to blame? Could its officers, such as John

H. Winder and Henry Wirz, have done anything to relieve the suffering at Anderson Station?

Those issues never go away; they come back to haunt this country in our treatment of captured combatants. Andersonville and the other Civil War prisons warn us of the perils of letting momentary fear, hate, expediency and partisan politics threaten to blind us to the traditional principles that we claim to embrace. A decision is only momentary, but the past and its consequences go on forever.

2

CAMP SUMTER BECOMES ANDERSONVILLE

With the exchange of prisoners having broken down and Richmond's prisons threatened, Captain William Sidney Winder received orders from the Confederate War Department to find a location for a new prison for civilians, sailors, white officers of black troops, privates and noncommissioned officers captured by the Southern military. The site needed to have access to a railroad for transporting prisoners in a place where minimal shelter could be created. It would need to be supplied by local farms. With the help of local commissary Uriah B. Harrold, he considered several specific sites in southwest Georgia, including the towns of Americus and Albany. In November 1863, he rejected most of the locations due to local political opposition. Other sites proved to be too isolated or risked attack by Federal cavalry raids from Florida.

Winder and Harrold finally chose a railroad platform on the Southwestern Railroad in what was then Sumter County but today is Macon County. Benjamin B. Dykes of Wilkinson County had taken over, in 1861, his father's job as the agent at the Anderson Station, where he owned land that would include today's town of Andersonville. He persuaded the Confederate agents to rent nearby land owned by Deputy Sheriff William Wesley Turner on a tributary of Sweetwater Creek for thirty dollars per month for the prison. Dykes himself received fifty dollars per month for leasing various buildings to the Confederacy. He continued as stationmaster until 1864.

Anderson Station could meet these needs for some nine thousand prisoners, but only barely. Even Spanish explorers had considered this

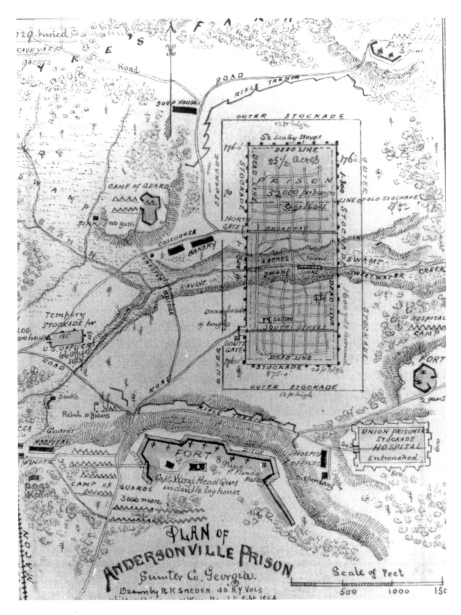

Prisoner Robert Knox Sneden drew this plan of Andersonville Prison from sketches and notes that he smuggled out of the prison. *Courtesy of the Virginia Historical Society.*

Camp Sumter Becomes Andersonville

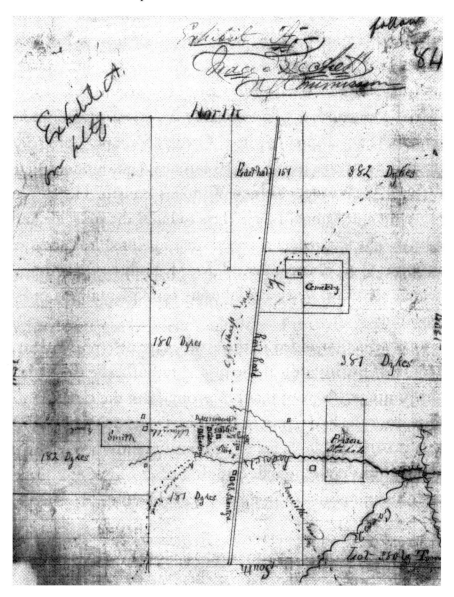

A map of the lands around Andersonville from the Civil War claim of Benjamin B. Dykes.
Courtesy of the National Archives and Records Administration.

flat plain a sparsely inhabited desert in 1540 and would have done so in 1863, too. It had only recently consisted of one log building used by the railroad. Between one to four families lived near Anderson Station, with a total population of twenty to seventy people. Railroad superintendent George W. Adams named this whistle-stop for Savannah entrepreneur John W. Anderson, and it still went by its original name as late as 1894. The United States Postal Department, however, designated its post office as Andersonville, as an Anderson post office already existed in Whitfield County, Georgia.

Dykes had sold the site by claiming that with so few people, there could be no serious objection to the prison. The people of Sumter County, however, loudly raised concerns about prisoners escaping, the Yankees encouraging slave revolts and even hungry guards raiding their farms, with or without official sanction. Ambrose Spencer lived near the prison and would later testify that many of his neighbors wanted to kill the prisoners to save rations for the Confederate army and end the threat of a mass escape. Brigadier General John H. Winder (Sidney's father), as commandant of the prison, would receive a letter from someone at Anderson Station that warned of the

Slaves being made to build a stockade for the Confederate government. *Courtesy of the Library of Congress.*

some three hundred prisoners working outside of the stockade organizing a mass escape. The Southern press reported on a group of alleged Southern guerillas appearing in Sumter County who may have actually been Federal soldiers. By June 24, Winder had a report that the civilians in the surrounding counties were stockpiling arms and plotting with Sherman to help in a mass escape. He supposedly turned back a party of civilians claiming to be bringing wagonloads of donated food for the prisoners, who by then numbered in the tens of thousands. If that incident actually did take place, the general may have suspected that it was somehow part of a breakout plot.

Building Camp Sumter, what would be known as Andersonville Prison, began on January 10, 1864, under the direction of Quartermaster Captain Richard Bayley Winder, Sidney Winder's cousin. English-born carpenter Samuel Leach Heys received the contract to build the stockade and administrative buildings. Nine hundred male and female slaves were impressed from farms and plantations in Sumter and Dougherty Counties and put to work under the direction of C.C. Sheppard and J.M. McNealy. Nails and other building materials proved to be scarce, and the later horrors of the prison began with its construction. Pine trees were cut down from the interior of the stockade to build the walls, with the intention of filling the space with barracks for shelter. The nearby sawmill owners refused to take contracts at government rates. Governor Joseph E. Brown and his political rival, Major General Howell Cobb, failed to win them over. The Confederate government finally ordered a sixty-day period wherein slaves and materials were confiscated for use in building the camp at official compensation. Tens of thousands of prisoners arrived and would leave, however, before any such buildings went up. The nearby unpainted Methodist church became a warehouse.

Richard Winder expanded the plans for the stockade to hold, not the 6,000 inmates originally intended, but as many as 9,000—and even that would prove far too inadequate. When Sergeant J.S. McGinley arrived at Anderson Station on February 24, he saw slave women still setting logs for the north wall of the stockade. He came as the first of some 40,000 prisoners to arrive at the prison. Prison trains brought 500 or more men at a time, to reach a high of 33,006 inmates by August 1864. During the worst months, the summer of 1864, the camp had a regular population of some 25,000 to 30,000 inmates. The Confederate government's bureaucracy failed to authorize the prison's officers to find the resources to feed and house the prisoners, but it could find the means to transport these thousands of men by train as a most extreme security measure.

That one of the greatest mass escapes in history did not occur in this prison in Sumter County can be largely credited to the work of its middle management officer, Captain Henry Wirz. When Andersonville accepted its first inmates in late February 1864, at a rate of some five hundred men per day, it had only an unfinished palisade of twenty-foot-high log uprights to separate them from the outside. Inmates could even reach out through gaps in the wall. A group of prisoners tried to undermine this simple barrier. The newly arrived Captain Henry Wirz, now in charge of the interior of the stockade, immediately ordered sentry towers, what the prisoners nicknamed "pigeon roosts," added to the top of the walls of the palisade.

Contrary to legend, the sentries shot few men, and the prisoners seem to have carried out few acts of malice against the guards. Even Americans used to squirreling guns and shotguns needed intense training to efficiently use the comparatively complex military weapons of the age. The guns, provided from the stores of the Macon Arsenal and chiefly used to threaten the prisoners, consisted of old flint and steel smoothbore muskets, including some from the Revolutionary War era, refitted for percussion. Some of the Georgia Reserves had knives, guns brought from home and pikes as armament.

At the time of the Civil War, the idea hardly existed of shooting individuals trying to breach, scale or tunnel a wall. On April 17, 1864, Brigadier General Winder ordered Wirz to establish the camp's infamous "dead line," a railing three feet high that marked an interior space fifteen feet from the stockade, similar to the security measures that existed in Northern prisons and as a picket line around any Civil War camp. In theory, prisoners who entered that area would be shot, although the antique weapons that the guards carried were almost useless at hitting a specific target. Innocent bystanders would have more likely been shot. Contrary to rumors believed by the prisoners, guards had no incentive to fire and could have been in trouble for shooting a prisoner without orders. Private James E. Anderson of the First Georgia Reserves described the guards as "trigger happy," in a letter to President Jefferson Davis, as did his fellow guard, Charles H. Thiot of Chatham County, when writing home. Historian William Marvel believes that no more than eleven men were killed by the sentries, and even fewer were wounded. More often than not, however, the sentries ignored prisoners passing in and out of the dead line area adjoining the walls. Guards would even encourage the inmates to approach the wall to trade.

The guards were major residents of this strange city—the fifth largest in what remained of the Confederate States of America in 1864—officially Camp Sumter but popularly and in legend the notorious Andersonville. If a flimsy palisade wall, earthworks and some cannons seemed so inadequate for holding back what came to be more than 30,000 prisoners, that most important of tasks had to fall to the garrison. Lieutenant Colonel D.T. Chandler reported that on August 5, 1864, Andersonville had 3,976 men to watch over some 25,000 prisoners. They were having a good day. Their numbers may have been as few as 1,000 to 1,200 men fit for duty, but whatever their total number, 303 men stood for duty during the day, but only 966 of the whole garrison could have been armed at any time. The inmates could outnumber the members of the garrison by a ratio of 100 to 1.

The first prisoners brought with them as guards the 400 remaining battle-hardened veterans of the Twenty-sixth Alabama Infantry Regiment. They were joined by the 270 men of the Fifty-fifth Georgia Infantry who escaped from or were not at that regiment's disastrous defeat at Cumberland Gap, Tennessee, on September 9, 1863. Together, the two units would have 250 to 300 men to guard as many as 13,000 men. The Fifty-seventh Georgia Infantry Regiment from Savannah and Gamble's Florida Light Artillery were added to the garrison in April 1864 to prevent a feared mass escape. The artillerymen, described as well disciplined, would remain at the prison, and they brought with them four pieces of artillery supplemented soon after with a battery of guns captured at the Battle of Olustee. Soldiers from other Confederate units would also find themselves at Anderson Station, usually as escorts for prisoners sent to Andersonville.

On May 15, all of the infantry left the prison for the front, except for the Fifty-fifth Georgia. The latter had been held in such low regard that its members were not wanted for the army. At Andersonville, the regiment could hardly muster one hundred men on any given day, even with new recruits from local men seeking to serve close to home. The Fifty-fifth soldiers were not used as guards on the prison's wall as it was reported that they threatened to join the prisoners in a mass escape.

After May 9, 1864, the bulk of the garrison and the guards would consist of Georgia Reserves regiments: the First under Colonel James H. Fannin, the Second under Colonel Robert F. Maddox, the Third under Colonel C.J. Harris and the Fourth under Colonel Robert S. Taylor. These regiments escorted prisoners being brought from Macon. Together, they belonged to

A postwar engraving of part of the garrison at Andersonville shows a Confederate flag, something that the prison never had. *Author's collection.*

Brigadier General Lucius J. Gartrell's Second Brigade, but they were usually commanded, when at Andersonville, by Colonel Fannin.

The reserves were notorious for having draft evaders and Union sympathizers who had lied about their respective ages to avoid conscription. Brigadier General John H. Winder, as post commandant at Andersonville, came to disapprove of the reserves and wanted to replace them with militia. They arrived at Andersonville without training, equipment or uniforms; many of the men did not even have shoes. Their skin was darkened from the sun and the smoke from the pine wood fires in the stockade. Like the prisoners, these soldiers became emaciated from hookworms. As their clothes became rags and they used blankets for coats, they eventually looked more and more like the prisoners and slave workers.

Myths about the guards of Andersonville have become better known than the men who spawned them, in part due to postwar claims by the men themselves. Jane Benson, however, has examined the records and found that almost none of these soldiers, contrary to legend, were boys or old men. In fact, few of the reserves were under age seventeen or older than forty-five. They were tall for their times, usually five feet, eight inches or taller, and generally, like most of the men of the Fifty-fifth, from poor Appalachian families in northern Georgia.

Andersonville would be the greatest adventure that most of these men would ever have. They would—for most of them, for the first and only time—be exposed to people, accents and language from throughout the United States and Europe. Men would form lifelong friendships with one another. Then and later, they would defend themselves, their prison and the reputation of Captain Wirz against charges of cruelty committed against his prisoners.

The guards, however, took on a terrible responsibility. Added to the myriad problems that the Confederacy inflicted on the people of the South, it inadvertently created a situation where only a comparatively few men manned a log wall that held back tens of thousands of desperate enemy soldiers. If freed, the starving, sick and desperate men, perhaps armed and accompanied by their former guards, could spread the horrors of Andersonville to thousands of farms across the state. Southern soldiers would then desert to protect their families or even join the marauders. Situations could have also been created, similar to the years in the South after the American Revolution, where such men would have even formed communities that lived from robbery and which would continue years after the war ended. As early as April 17, 1864, the disgruntled guards nearly rioted. Often, they became sick from exposure to the camp, and they reportedly suffered a strange facial malady, likely some form of "camp itch," from exposure to the air of the stockade. Even General Winder came down with what his doctors diagnosed as "gangrene of the face." He was told, as a consequence, to cease entering the stockade. Poor rations and disease decimated their ranks, although contrary to legend, their mortality rate never rose to close to matching that of the prisoners. Records show that as many as one-third of the men would be recorded as sick at one time. A total of 226 guards died at Andersonville, with 117 of that number buried there, including 43 listed as (name) unknown.

Guard duty also proved almost as monotonous as being a prisoner and encouraged the escape of guards, as well as prisoners. Members of the garrison would claim that service at Andersonville became worse than time in the regular army. Each day of having to face overwhelming numbers of desperate enemy soldiers, and under abominable conditions, stressed out the relatively few men charged with stopping the world's greatest mass escape. Yankee-born Weld Hamlin provides one example. Impressment officers found him trying to hide in the Florida swamps in order to avoid serving in the Confederate army against his brothers in the North. Hamlin became a guard at Andersonville as an alternative to imprisonment. Eventually, he deserted, choosing hiding, capture, prison and a fugitive's life to continuing to serve at Camp Sumter.

Some of these soldiers would disappear for days and return with little note made of their absence. As the war crossed north Georgia, many of these troops, fearing for the safety of their families, deserted. Colonel Fannin later testified of liberally granting leaves so that his men could go home and farm. Likely, this policy discouraged his men from just leaving forever. Members of the reserves also frequently left in details to work as mechanics for the government or to serve as scouts for the Confederate armies in Georgia. The camp adjutant, Lieutenant James Ormond of the Second Georgia Reserves, had been a successful Atlanta merchant. When Sherman occupied that city, Ormond passed through the Federal lines to learn that while his home was being used as a Federal headquarters, the Yankees had treated his family well. He reciprocated by returning to Andersonville with a blanket, a shelter tent and fifty dollars in Confederate money for a prisoner relation of a Federal officer.

Desertions thus became a serious threat to the camp's security. In early October, the Macon newspapers published the names of hundreds of the reserves who were absent without leave. Most of them came from counties occupied or threatened by the Federal army, although the lists included names of men from counties near Andersonville and from areas in northeast Georgia untouched by the war. During the great transfer of prisoners from Andersonville to other camps, the reserves, along with many of the prisoners, took advantage of the train trip to escape. General Winder wrote in July 1864 that twelve of his men had left without leave and that he feared that all would follow immediately. If inmate Lawrence LeBron did kill a guard and dump the body in a creek during his escape, the missing Confederate soldier likely appeared on the rolls as a deserter. A corporal's guard began searching trains leaving Anderson Station for deserters. The camp's dog packs chased deserters from the garrison, as well as the prisoners.

As Camp Sumter lacked a general court-martial for much of its history, the guards rarely suffered punishment. The officers likely also took unauthorized absences. In any case, they likely tried to encourage their men to return. Officially, guards could suffer the same disciplines as the inmates, except for confinement on the chain gang. In reality, a guard would only stand on a box for a couple of hours, if punished at all. Certainly, the camp lacked professional officers and soldiers to serve as examples for the garrison. D.M. Pass of Gordon County, formerly of the Fourth Reserves, would claim, many years after the war, that he helped a condemned deserter and friend named Knight to escape. He identified the prisoners as Federals but he was more likely referring to two men from the Fifty-fifth Georgia. Furthermore, any punishment inflicted on a guard could hardly have been worse than the circumstances of doing service at Anderson Station.

Most of the prisoners and their remaining guards left Andersonville for other prisons in September 1864. This move prevented the rescue of the inmates by Sherman's cavalry. The Fifth Georgia Reserves (Lieutenant Colonel Christopher Findlay) arrived from Macon to help with the evacuation. The First, Third and Fourth Reserves, along with most of the artillery, would help to garrison the new Camp Lawton at Millen, Georgia. At least some of those men would also battle Sherman's legions in South Carolina. Members of the First and Fourth would eventually return to Andersonville, after Millen had to be abandoned, with the prisoners who had been transferred to Blackshear, Georgia, an open-air prison on an island where conditions were even worse than at Andersonville. The reserves helped in the general exchange and release of prisoners that began in March 1865. The Fifty-fifth Georgia escorted prisoners to Florence, South Carolina, and would end the war guarding prisoners in North Carolina. A detachment from the regiment under Captain Chapman defended Savannah and opposed the Yankee march through the Carolinas.

More extreme measures were needed to stop escapes than the artillery and the antique weapons of the guards. At night, dog packs and mounted guards circled the stockade. The grounds were illuminated by pine knot fires, as the guards in the towers proved their vigilance by regularly calling out to one another. To enforce respect among the inmates, the garrison would occasionally parade or fire a cannon shot or two into the swamp at the center of the stockade. Eventually, cannons and forts were positioned to sweep the interior of the overcrowded stockade in the case that the desperate prisoners tried a mass escape or if Federal troops arrived to stage a rescue.

The dogs belonged to Private Edward C. Turner and had been trained to hunt raccoons, opossums and escaped slaves. He organized packs of some five animals each with a leader that was at least part bloodhound. These animals could be fooled by the nearby Flint River, slave paths or rain; they could also run past escaped prisoners without catching their scent. Contrary to accounts in prisoner memoirs, no firsthand account has been found of these mongrels attacking anyone. Trained to find but not harm escaped slaves, the dogs played with the prisoners they tracked down while waiting for the arrival of the amiable Turner and the guards.

The Andersonville guards also used demonstrations of force to squelch planned mass escapes by the prisoners in April, May and July. Workmen physically strengthened the stockade to prevent the prisoners from pushing it down. On July 28, the camp gunners fired a cannon shot into the marsh in the middle of the camp as a warning to the prisoners. The next day, additional areas within the stockade were marked with white flags to indicate where artillery would disperse any large gatherings of prisoners. A severe thunderstorm on August 9 created gaps in the wall. General Winder flew into a panic and called out the militia. By then, the inmates were in such a weakened condition, however, that they made no effort at an escape. They instead huddled together and pleaded with the garrison not to open fire.

The security measures had a basis in more than paranoia. Rebel leaders believed that Rousseau's cavalry had intended to release the Andersonville captives in July 1864. General Sherman's horsemen later made a failed effort to rescue the prisoners at Macon and Andersonville. The women around Andersonville were evacuated.

The prison's garrison became part of the greater legend of Andersonville. Among its officers, Colonel James H. Fannin and Lieutenant Colonel Alexander W. Persons testified to the service of the garrison at the trial of Andersonville's Captain Henry Wirz. The most often repeated account of the guards first appeared in 1874, nine years after the prison closed. The account's author, Lemuel Madison Park, served at Andersonville in the First Georgia Reserves. He made wildly inaccurate, but still often repeated, statements in defense of the Confederate treatment of Federal prisoners. For example, he wrongly described his fellow guards as little better than boys and old men who died at the same rate as the prisoners. Park claimed to have been a fifteen-year-old boy when he served at the prison. In fact, he enlisted at age seventeen and turned eighteen as a guard. The problems created by his memoir became worse when they were later combined with other misinformation published in partisan prisoner memoirs and popular fiction, such as Herbert Collingwood's novel, *Andersonville Violets*, wherein the writer described the guards largely from his imagination.

As months went by, the garrison and the prisoners, men from very different worlds, merged into one culture, if not one people, all of whose members dreamed of getting away to anywhere else. This population of garrison, slave workers and prisoners had all of the characteristics of a major city, except for women and children, including merchants, thieves, gamblers, smugglers, watch repairmen and at least one counterfeiter. Space was sold just as real estate would be in any city.

Among the many improvements that Captain Wirz made after his arrival in late March 1864 was organizing the men into messes and squads for purposes of maintaining a roll and issuing rations. The identities of many of these men have not survived. Some prisoners likely ignored roll call out of spite or so that their families would never know that they died at Andersonville. Surviving lists of the prisoners are largely of the names of the men who died, worked in the hospital or left the stockade by any means. Prisoners assumed false identities to gain extra rations, to hide from prosecution for desertion/reenlisting in order to fraudulently receive extra bounty money and to falsely claim to belong to groups that received special exchanges, such as sailors or Sherman's cavalrymen. Escaping under the name of another prisoner came to be called "flanking out." Researcher Jack Lundquist identified 631 men buried in the camp's cemetery for whom no service records exists, and 1,205 men reported as having died in the prison but without identified graves. Deducting the 533 graves of unknown dead, there are still 672 men unaccounted for.

The greatest tale of Andersonville identity theft involved Jacques Roellinger, a deserter from the French army. He came to the United States in 1862 and enlisted in the Enfants Perdues ("Lost Children") New York Independent Infantry Battalion, a unit of French and Italian nationals derisively called the "Lost Ducks" for the sounds of their accents. Roellinger deserted only days later, he claimed, from a fear that if France became an ally of the Confederacy and he fell into enemy hands, he would be extradited and executed by his native country. Nonetheless, on the advice of his brother, he joined the 107th Ohio Infantry Regiment under the name of Jacques Cermann.

In the meantime, another man took advantage of Roellinger's desertion and assumed his identity in the Enfants Perdues, a common practice in this battalion of men with questionable pasts. This new recruit suffered capture at the Battle of Olustee, Florida, on February 20, 1864, and ended up at Andersonville, where he died from scorbutus (scurvy) on August 22, 1864. Prisoner Frederick Guscetti, a former member of the Enfants Perdues who had transferred to the Forty-seventh New York Infantry Regiment only to suffer near death at Olustee, took over the dead imposter's false identity as Roellinger. At Andersonville, he went by the name of Frado and "Little Frenchy." Using that nickname, this man became Andersonville's most inept and unsuccessful escape artist, until he escaped in March 1865 while on his way to an exchange of prisoners that he mistakenly believed to be a Confederate ruse. After the war, he tried to testify at the trial of Henry Wirz to repay the Confederate's kindness in arranging his exchange, only to be barred for trying to raise money for Wirz's defense.

After the war, Guscetti applied for back pay and other compensation under his own name, as well as under the identity of Jacques Roellinger. With a small boy he claimed as a son, he also persuaded the secretary of war that, as Roellinger, his death had been incorrectly reported at Andersonville. Drawing pensions as both Guscetti and Roellinger, he also filed for a pension, with himself listed as a witness, as the father of a deceased Jacques Roellinger who was shot and killed by the guards at Andersonville in August 1864. In another pension application, a woman filed a pension claim as Roellinger's widow. A chance meeting by pension attorneys exposed the frauds and resulted in Guscetti being sentenced to seven years in prison. He would eventually return to his native Italy, and from there he, and later his widow, successfully applied for Federal pensions for his real service as Guscetti. The real Jacques Roellinger also received a pension after having to explain his desertion and false identity.

Prisoner Solon Hyde of the Seventeenth Ohio Infantry made exploring this prison and understanding these men his pastime. Among the prisoners, he found all characters, as well as communities of all races, languages and nationalities, serving in the Federal military. The prison population included some of the first Italians, Slavs and Portuguese to arrive in America. Seemingly everyone at Andersonville who was not a native of the United States, a German or an Irishman went by the nickname "Frenchy." All states had representatives, including at least one Georgia soldier. Even California had representation, through members who had come east and enlisted in the Second Massachusetts Cavalry. Hyde found that the single men tended to last longer than did husbands and fathers. Members of the Odd Fellows and Masonic fraternities received special aid from their respective brothers inside and outside of the prison.

While Andersonville never achieved Governor John B. Gordon's claim of it being no worse than a third-rate hotel (Gordon never saw the prison), or as one old veteran would relate after the war, not as bad as living with his wife's

Barbers Shops in the Stockade.

Just near my tent is a barber shop. The owner lives, or exists in a sunken shanty. He has a barber pole too - made of a long stick with the bark cut out in serpentine shape like any barber pole in a City -

old Blanket

A Barber's Shop.

Some of the prisoners who last came in managed to secrete the razors somehow. Everything else was taken from them by Wirz at his headquarters on the hill before they were marched in the gate.— The barbers do a good business on fine warm days only. We have been having very cold blustry weather for nearly a week - Several have died from hunger and exposure. As hundreds have no shelter at all only the ragged clothes on their backs - They mope all day and night over little fires. all are woe begone. ragged. dirty. and black with pitch pine smoke

Andersonville had all of the qualities of a major city in 1864 except for a lack of women and children. Prisoner Robert Knox Sneden drew these postwar sketches of places familiar to all of the prison's population. *Courtesy of the Virginia Historical Society.*

cats, it did become more than survivable for a few of the prisoners, especially compared to life and death in the camps and battlefields where they had served. Some three hundred white prisoners were needed for various work details at any given time, and they were rewarded with double rations and freedom to stay outside of the stockade. They would rob local gardens, and by that means William Lugenbeal claimed he actually got fat. William Smith, also on the work details, lived in a cabin, had access to newspapers, read books, played baseball and socialized with ladies. He helped to organize a mock presidential debate and a mock election that Lincoln won, all with the permission of Captain Wirz. When he finally obtained an exchange as a sick prisoner, he took baggage with him.

Other prisoners survived by enlisting in the Confederate army in Colonel J.G. O'Neil's Tenth Tennessee Confederate Infantry Regiment and also in a defense force that likely helped in the defense of Savannah from General

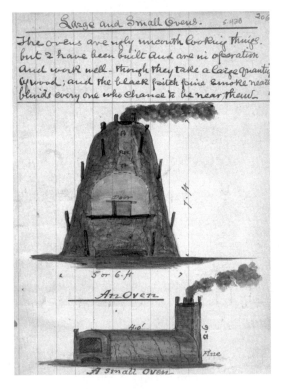

This page and next: Andersonville had all of the qualities of a major city in 1864, except for a lack of women and children. Prisoner Robert Knox Sneden drew these postwar sketches of places familiar to all of the prison's population. *Courtesy of the Virginia Historical Society.*

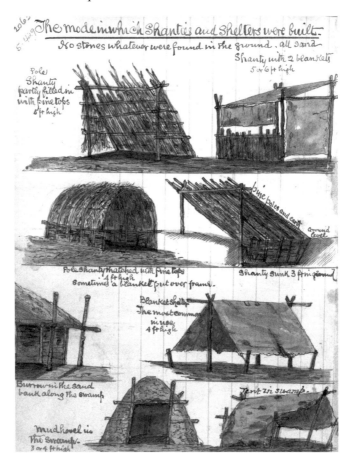

THE WATCHMAKER'S SHANTY.

Sherman. Many of O'Neil's "galvanized Yankees," men whose uniforms, like hot steel, changed from blue to gray with their new service, were later captured at the Battle of Egypt Station, Mississippi. They then became inmates of a Federal prison, where they enlisted back into the Union army to protect settlers in the West from Indians. Legends started that some of these men would receive both Confederate pensions from the State of Tennessee and Federal pensions from the United States government.

The new prison did begin with a positive reputation. Prisoners heard the reports in Southern newspapers about Andersonville and fought for the opportunity to escape hunger, disease and exposure at Belle Island in Richmond. The first prisoners were, initially, not disappointed. They found the climate a pleasant change from the winter weather of Virginia. Reporters complimented the prisoners on building their own huts. This massive transfer of prisoners from Richmond with only a minimal amount of preparation at a site inadequate to support such numbers of people, however, created the Andersonville Prison of legend—the largest prison of the Civil War and one of America's greatest disasters.

Determining the exact number of men who entered Andersonville has proven problematic. The statistics from Captain Wirz's morning reports are highly suspect, as men allowed themselves to be counted twice for extra rations in the camp's two daily roll calls. Furthermore, historian William Marvel has pointed out that some men were returned to the prison at least once, if not twice. Rolls of the prisoners, when they survive at all, have the same problems of false and stolen identities. The late Jack Lundquist carefully compiled rolls of Union Civil War prisoners of war and estimated that the total number for Andersonville likely fell to just under forty thousand individual prisoners.

The railroad made creating such an installation possible, but it failed to supply a population large enough to be the Confederacy's fifth-largest city. One prisoner remembered Anderson Station as only four or five rickety wood plank buildings and some twenty equally decrepit residents. Eventually, it grew to have two saloons, a blacksmith shop, a Methodist church, general stores and some dozen houses. Prisoners traded their belongings to the guards, who in turn sold the same to the merchants of this ad hoc boomtown for food traded back to the inmates. This trade saved the lives of thousands of the inmates at Andersonville. Prisoners taken at Plymouth, North Carolina, in April 1864 were allowed to keep their pay and personal belongings, some $1 million in tradable cash and goods. Prisoner "Old Jimmie Bowlegs"

This post–Civil War print of Andersonville Prison shows the town that grew up around Anderson Station and prospered on the wealth generated by the guards and prisoners. *Courtesy of the Library of Congress.*

started with only a button, but he traded up so successfully that when he left the prison in March 1865, he had $3,000 in cash. Inmate George W. Fechter justified his being one of the largest such merchants by helping less fortunate prisoners. Others wrote of prisoners being gouged by such "swindlers," who grew rich while their comrades, left with nothing to trade, starved, sickened and died at their feet.

So many people from so many different places brought together under such circumstances created experiences that became the subject of numerous memoirs, some even falsely written by persons who weren't there, and even more legends. MacKinlay Kantor would use those memoirs (the prison had no balanced history until 1968) as source material for his Pulitzer Prize–winning novel *Andersonville* (1955). He stayed within the facts better than some memoirists and historians.

This strange gathering of people at the Anderson Station railroad siding included among the prisoners numerous suspicious characters suspected of being Federal spies or worse, including Ann Williams of Liberty County,

Georgia. Captain Wirz had her arrested for having carnal knowledge with no fewer than seven of the prisoners. Lorenzo T. Potter of Charleston, South Carolina, on behalf of his wife, Eliza, bribed Confederate officials to ship supplies to the prisoners at Andersonville. Some women in the neighborhood of the prison tried to ease the suffering in the camp, such as Lucy Herrington, who carried food to the sick prisoners. In January 1865, Wirz wrote of a suspicious Mrs. Spaulding from Americus whose husband played a prominent role in a local Unionist meeting. She came to visit a Federal soldier from nearby Americus who had traveled north at the beginning of the war, married there and enlisted in Dubuque in an Iowa regiment. He had smuggled a letter out of the prison by way of a friend among the guards. Mrs. Spaulding had been in the North. She brought back the reply as a family friend while also inquiring about buying Federal currency from the prisoners. A Mary Rawson of nearby Plains also regularly visited a Peter Kiene of the Sixteenth Iowa and brought him food baskets.

The most famous character involved with Andersonville was Captain Henry Wirz himself. In legend, and at his later war crimes trial, he would be portrayed as the commander of the prison and a monster that shot, or ordered shot, almost at random, helpless prisoners. Wirz, however, portrayed himself as a disabled veteran of battle who had no authority to ease the sufferings of the prisoners and who had harmed no one.

The real Hartmann Heinrich "Henry" Wirz does not fit either version. Never the commandant of the prison, he likely held his lowly position as chief clerk because of his success as an administrator at Cahawba Prison and out of General Winder's sympathy for the real or imagined debilitating injury in his arm. He would be gone from the post on leave in an effort to find treatment, although he claimed to be a homeopathic doctor, and an autopsy would later fail to find anything wrong with him. Inmates would believe rumors that the emasculated captain had died.

As an experienced prison keeper and protégé of General Winder, Wirz did try to improve conditions at Andersonville after his arrival in March 1864. With no support or resources, the captain managed to lay out streets, organized prisoners into messes, attempted to improve sanitation and compiled rolls of the prisoners. Many prisoners remembered his kindness to them, and others, including men who had violated their oaths not to escape from work details, would write of suffering no worse punishment than his abusive foul language. The camp did have stocks, chains and dog packs, but credible accounts describe these "punishments" for prisoners who had promised not to escape as brief, only inconvenient and hardly more than annoying, not fatal. In addition to the fact that the two pistols Wirz carried as he rode alone among the prisoners on his gray horse did not work, he never ordered anyone shot or executed.

As early as 1865, however, some prisoners complained of his brutality and said that he showed partiality to fellow immigrants from Germanic Europe. Then and later, that image of Wirz likely came about because almost none of the prisoners had met any other Confederate officer besides him. They wrongly assumed that he was in command of the whole post and thereby somehow responsible for all of their suffering. His actual authority extended to hardly more than being able to delay the serving of rations until the rolls were taken and deciding who could and could not enter or leave the stockade. At that time, xenophobic prejudices ran high in America against German Roman Catholic immigrants. That the Catholic convert Wirz spoke English with a German accent that betrayed his Swiss birth did not help his image. Confederate inspectors, however, praised him for his energy and efficiency, especially when compared to the camp's other officers, and recommended him for promotion.

None of the inmates became more legendary than the women of Andersonville. Some female Georgians helped prisoners escape, while others made successful captures of fugitives. Women also could become prisoners, and not just as female soldiers who had enlisted as men and who sometimes died without their sex and true identities being known. Wives would follow civilian and soldier husbands into the war and sometimes to capture. Prisoner Edward Wellington Boate testified to seeing two women inmates of Andersonville, Margaret Leonard and Francis Jane Hunt. Twenty-eight-year-old Irish servant Margaret Larney, captured with her husband, Isaac Newton Leonard, at Plymouth, North Carolina, on April 20, 1864, found herself at Andersonville. As a laundress, she would be remembered for continuing to cook for the soldiers even while under fire. She remained behind at Plymouth for four weeks while she nursed the sick. Eventually, she and her husband were taken to Andersonville. Margaret arrived at the prison camp in a hog cart, but although she was treated with kindness during her odyssey, she stayed there only ten days. Captain Wirz tried to use her as a maid but she proved so disagreeable that he had her transferred to Richmond, where she was soon after exchanged. Isaac and Margaret Leonard survived the war, although he never recovered from his prison experience and died in Springfield, Massachusetts, about 1869. Margaret moved to Kernville, California, with their son, George, and died there about 1900.

The only other documented female prisoner at Andersonville gave birth to the prison's only child. Chicagoan Francis Jane "Janie" Scadin had married ship captain Herbert Henry Hunt. Sometime before June 1864, the Hunts were captured by the Confederate home guard with Herbert's ship at Fairfield, North Carolina. For reasons unknown, the Hunts remained at Andersonville until the prison all but closed, during which time Janie Hunt gave birth to a son, believed to have been named Frank, on July 9, 1864. The baby apparently died between February 3, 1865, and when the Hunts left the prison on April 15, 1865.

Much about the Hunts remains a mystery and suggests that they went into hiding for decades. This family cannot be found in the 1870 and 1880 federal censuses. Herbert had previously served in the army before receiving a medical discharge but he made no effort to obtain a Federal pension in his later years. John H. Morris, the owner of Hunt's ship, was captured with it and also went to Andersonville. He would pass through the lines, buying and selling checks and securities from desperate prisoners at great personal profit. His ship and cargo may have been bought with money from shady investors in New York. Morris may have then betrayed his ship to the Confederacy only to claim the value of it and its cargo as a captured prize while telling his investors that he had lost the ship and its cargo. The Hunts may have been caught in the middle of Morris's schemes and feared either Federal prosecutor or Morris, or Morris's former partners. The Hunts would later live in the Newark-Communipaw area of New Jersey although they later moved to Rocky Hill, Connecticut, where Janie passed away in 1894 and Herbert died in 1926.

Boate may not have known of all of the female prisoners of Andersonville. A story that appeared in the *Memphis Daily Appeal* on May 14, 1864, before the Hunts arrived at Andersonville, mentioned one of the camp's five female prisoners giving birth. She may have been the Mrs. Baxter remembered by one prisoner as having been captured down the Mississippi. Legends tell of women hidden among the soldiers who were discovered when giving birth or found among the dead, stripped of clothing by needy prisoners. Many or all such tales are likely fiction, refer to other prisons or come from the stories of Leonard and Hunt.

Confusion also exists over the legendary Roman Catholic priests who served the prisoners of Andersonville. In May 1864, Father William John Hamilton, while attending to his mission church in Americus, Georgia, visited Andersonville for a few hours to see if he could be of service. The following week, he spent three more days at the prison and then wrote to his superior, Bishop Augustan Verot, about the horrors he had found and the need for priests among the inmates. His Grace would twice visit the prison himself, and he dispatched, at different times, Peter Whelan, Henry Peter Clavreul, Peter Dufau, John F. Kirby and Anselm Usannaz to meet this need. Father Whelan, a former Confederate chaplain who spent time in a Northern prison, served the longest time at Andersonville, although he would be confused in the prison lore with Hamilton. He also borrowed $16,000 to purchase flour for the sick inmates, an act for which the United States government later declined to reimburse him.

Aside from the above priests, the inmates met almost all of Andersonville's other religious needs. Literally mad from being a hatter, religious zealot Sergeant Thomas H. "Boston" Corbett became something of prophet in the apocalyptical environment of Andersonville. With Sergeants Benjamin N. Waddell, Thomas J. Sheppard and others, he led religious and patriotic meetings that raised morale and saved lives. Corbett, however, would win Civil War fame only later and as the man who killed John Wilkes Booth. He escaped from a Kansas insane asylum in 1888 and survived hostile winter weather to reach Mexico and legend.

The stories of such people, and even the words on the original contemporary documents, lead one to visualize a place almost more imaginary than real. Seeing Andersonville as a real place, as a writer for the *Richmond Whig* in 1865 noted, required photographs of it when it neared its peak in overcrowding, before Wirz arranged for improvements that hid it at its worst.

Andrew J. Riddle, a Macon, Georgia photographer, supplied that need and left for posterity what would be rare photographs for any Civil War prison: life images of a day in the deadliest of those places of confinement. Without his work, the only visuals from the camp to survive would have been sensationalized drawings made by the prisoners and the postwar government photographs of John F. Engle and James Furlong of Fernandina, Florida.

Like seemingly everyone connected with that place, Riddle had a colorful history of his own. Born in New Castle County, Delaware, on February 28, 1828, as the child of John and Sarah Riddle, he became involved with photography in 1846, likely by studying under a friend, the famed lithographer Napoleon Sarony of New York. Riddle had opened his own photography studio in Baltimore, Maryland, by 1851. The following year, he and his elderly mother lived in his studio in Columbus, Georgia. By 1856, Andrew had obtained the rights to use and teach Jeremiah Gurney's "hallotype" process of creating colored ambrotypes that had a three dimensional effect. That October, he studied under well-known Boston photographer J.A. Whipple. In the 1860 census, the Riddles appeared as residents of both Macon and Rome, Georgia.

After the war began, Andrew J. Riddle opened a studio at 151 Main Street in Richmond, Virginia. In October 1862, Federal authorities arrested him in Charles County, Maryland, when he tried to smuggle a trunk load of photographic supplies from Washington to his new studio in Richmond. The Union provost marshal seized Riddle's goods but allowed him to continue on to Richmond. The following April, he tried to obtain a pass to move through the Confederate lines to his native Maryland. By September 25, 1863, Riddle had served four months of what became an eight-month prison term imposed by the Federals for trying to smuggle still more photographic supplies, this time from New York through Westmoreland County, Virginia. By July 1864, he had returned to Macon, where he was conscripted as a private in the Confederate engineers.

In addition to reproducing maps for the army, Riddle worked as chief photographer for the western armies under General Joseph E. Johnston. (Johnston also later became a resident of Macon.) As the Confederacy's only verified official photographer, he made a now-famous photograph of the ironclad CSS *Jackson* with views of the new ordnance buildings in Macon. He mass-produced maps for the army using the photographic method developed by Major Albert H. Campbell in Richmond. The Campbell process used photographs, tracing paper and sunlight in a crude but effective version of the modern photo duplication process.

On August 16, 1864, Riddle photographed scenes in and around the Andersonville stockade. In one of the endless ironies associated with that place, a man who had himself been a prisoner of war for smuggling photography supplies now used his camera to record images of his former captor's soldiers and sailors held in the greatest prison of the world. He photographed the prisoners in such a way that he created a story line of life and burial at Andersonville. During that day, he made seven prints of the interior of the stockade, one of the cemetery and another of a burial detail in the prison cemetery. For whatever reason, he failed to make a complete series of images by including the removal of the dead and the hospital. Riddle also made at least two portraits during this trip, one of Brigadier General John T. Winder, commandant of the camp and commander of all prisons east of the Mississippi, and another of Captain Henry Wirz. Riddle developed and dated the prints of the prison the next day.

Riddle had taken the only surviving photographs of Federal inmates in an operating Confederate prison. On the day Riddle photographed Andersonville, more than one hundred inmates died from starvation, disease and exposure; six thousand men already lay buried in the cemetery; and twenty-five hundred others waited for what little medical attention the camp's staff could provide. Riddle's camera recorded a sea of tents, some huts and even the holes in the ground used by the inmates. He took three of the views from where rain had created a large gap in the wall on the east side. The storm that had torn down a section of the wall had been a blessing, breaking a drought and exposing the so-called Providence Spring, a previously unknown, covered source of clean water as an alternative to the marshy creek near the south end of the camp.

The photographs quickly became part of the larger legend of Andersonville. During the trial of Andersonville officer Henry Wirz, the judge advocate announced that he planned to introduce into evidence a group of photographs of the prison. He was likely referring to Andrew J. Riddle's work. Ambrose C. Spencer used an engraving from a Riddle photograph in his *A Narrative of Andersonville* (1866).

New York Yankee civilian Ambrose Spencer lived near the prison. He included this illustration of the interior of the prison in his bestselling book on the trial of Andersonville's Captain Henry Wirz. If Spencer ever saw the prison, he likely only did so while a militiaman called up to supplement the guards. *Author's collection.*

Riddle's photographic process produced only prints. Before the war, however, he had invented a camera that made two photographs at once. One set of his Andersonville prints went to the camp's officials and the other set Riddle retained. After the war, Riddle displayed his complete set of Andersonville pictures and eventually sold them to former prisoner of war Daniel S. Camp. Robert H. Kellogg, another Andersonville inmate alumnus, had seen Riddle make the photographs on August 16, 1864, and later saw the photographer trying to sell his set of the prints in New York in June 1865. Kellogg acquired the photographs and donated them to the State Library of Connecticut in 1922. He did not donate them to the federal government because he had been warned that souvenir hunters often stole photographs from the War Department. The Kellogg set of prints has been copied and published many times, including for the holdings of the U.S. Army Military History Institute at Carlisle Barracks, Pennsylvania.

In October 1865, Theodore Wiseman moved near Anderson Station and found seven of the Riddle photographs in Captain Wirz's trunk. He would display them at veterans' meetings for years afterward. In 1883, as a

This and next five pages: Confederate military photographer Andrew J. Riddle recorded the living and the dead at Andersonville on August 16, 1864, creating an extremely rare view of a Civil War prison during the war. *Courtesy of the Hargrett Rare Book and Manuscripts Library, University of Georgia Libraries.*

Camp Sumter Becomes Andersonville

resident of Lawrence, Kansas, Wiseman had the photographs copyrighted and published. He then sold complete sets of the prints for two dollars. The War Department had acquired a copy of the photographs by 1897. Today, the National Archives and Records Administration has that copy. Other sets

of the Riddle prints survive in the holdings of the Hargrett Rare Book and Manuscripts Library of the University of Georgia Libraries.

In the interim, Riddle had the good fortune of being in Macon to photograph one of the symbolic moments of the end of the Civil War. From a window, he made the now often reproduced photograph of the arrival of the wagon train carrying Confederate president Jefferson Davis as a prisoner of the Federal government. Davis had been arrested by cavalry at Irwinville, Georgia, on May 10, 1865, within a day's journey of the by then abandoned Andersonville prison. Davis missed seeing it, but for the rest of his life, the Confederate president would defend his lost nation against charges of cruelty to prisoners at Andersonville.

Andrew J. Riddle would continue his photographic career in Columbus, Eufaula and Macon, sometimes achieving attention for his work in life-size prints, colorization and studio backgrounds. He failed to accumulate capital or to overcome his problems with gambling and alcohol. Andrew J. Riddle died in Columbus on March 21, 1897, and was buried at Rose Hill Cemetery in Macon two days later.

3

The Horror

Whole books have been published that use Andersonville as a case study in systems failure, but those works do not set it in the context of the greater shortcomings of the Confederate States of America. The new nation's bureaucracy lacked everything from adequately trained administrators to paper and ink, but it came by its shortcomings honestly. Aside from having to create a national government from scratch, it would not have had any historical experience in government operations on the scale it needed beyond the prewar national postal system. Fighting a modern war with an agricultural economy, limited population, inadequate transportation, corruption, drought, an enslaved labor force, states' rights obstructionist politics, few professionally trained administrators and other debilitating factors created a crisis for soldiers, civilians and prisoners of war across the Southern nation. The United States also had fatal system failures from 1861 to 1865, but much greater resources covered its many mistakes and even created an expanded, efficient and more diverse economy.

What organizational resources the Confederate government could muster had to be devoted to its most immediate crisis, to stopping the ever-advancing Federal military, breaking the blockade of the Southern ports and preventing a mass escape of the tens of thousands of prisoners being held in the capital of Richmond. Consequently, the lack of food, clothing and shelter at Belle Island and other Confederate prisons would only be moved to and made worse at the isolated Anderson Station in deep southwest Georgia. Desperate circumstances created this disaster, and the continuing failures of the Southern government kept anything from being done about it until the approaching war again forced the removal of the prisoners, for reasons of security, to, initially, a new and much-improved prison.

Almost all of the 12,949 Andersonville inmates buried today in its cemetery died from the effects of exposure, malnutrition, disease and declining morale. The Confederate government's intention that the new prison be built in a place with abundant foodstuffs, security and adequate housing was abandoned in the name of local political expediency. Civilian suppliers often sold only the poorest-quality foodstuffs to the government. Administrative failure and inadequate transportation allowed supplies to pile up at railroad stations, which waited for trains that never came or for the advancing Federal armies. Lieutenant Colonel Alexander W. Persons, Andersonville's first commandant, scrounged the South for food and materials to finish the camp. Shortly after the prison opened, the Confederate Congress unintentionally made matters worse with a law that transferred the supply problem to the commissary, Lieutenant John H. Wright of the Fifty-fifth Georgia Infantry. He could only make requests for cornmeal and salt pork from the distant military depots at Columbus, Albany and Macon. District commissary Captain A.M. Allen found beef so scarce that pork reserved for the army had to be sent to Andersonville instead. Florida's depleted wild cattle herds were expensive to obtain and so malnourished that they were almost worthless. Captain Henry Wirz, an officer charged with the prisoners, complained of the almost inedible quality of the food and the lack of utensils with which to serve it. A prison bakery was begun, but each day half of the camp's population received raw food, and even when cooked, the meal could be so coarse as to be inedible. Constant escapes from wood-gathering details limited the number of cooking fires. The depletion of the area's hardwood trees by the railroad left the camp under a perpetual pine smoke and the now dark "smoked Yanks" covered in soot.

Hunger became such a problem that no stores could be created, and a single train would make the difference for everyone, garrison, slaves and prisoners, eating or not. Prison officials ordered passing trains raided for food consigned to the army. Brigadier General John H. Winder, Alexander's successor as commandant of Andersonville, famously wrote of having 29,400 prisoners, 2,650 soldiers and 500 black laborers but not one ration. Prisoners dug for roots, risked their lives to kill swallows on the dead line at dusk and ate rats to stave off starvation. Extra rations could also be obtained by theft, working on a labor detail, packages from home or trade. Prisoners of war exchanged whatever they had with the guards, but this commerce gradually depleted and drove up the prices of the local food sources—too limited to have adequately fed the garrison, even under the best of circumstances. Stories were told of the prison's guards hijacking passing trains for food.

Individuals became skin and bones on the little cornmeal, beans, rice and meat rations that the Confederacy provided. Starving prisoners obsessed, talked and dreamed about food to the point that they would lose any will to live. Prisoner Solon Hyde found that the single men tended to last longer than did husbands and fathers with families to worry over. He also discovered that the naturally large, stout and robust died more often than the small and wiry soldiers. Native Americans died at a high rate due, in part, to being unable to accept captivity.

This empty wilderness gave confinement a particularly hellish quality, as men sent there after several days of a bleak train ride could come to believe that they had been sent to the end of the earth and forgotten. In prisons like Richmond's Belle Island, the inmates could see people moving about, hear distant cannon fire and at least speculate on what was occurring. At Andersonville, they could be punished just for talking to the slave workers. Some of the inmates, according to Thomas Hinds of the First Maryland Infantry and others, became "idiots and were peevish and childish." Prisoners would give up and lie down to die by the marsh that filled the center of the pen. Inmates received punishment for even talking to slaves and prisoners paroled to work outside the stockade. For this reason, Catholic priest Peter Whelan avoided sharing news with the men he came to help. Some information on the war did come in with new prisoners and from newspapers smuggled into the camp by Ransom "Little Red Cap" T. Powell, a drummer boy allowed to work at the camp's headquarters. Within the closed society held captive at Anderson Station, however, its members could come to feel as if the only world that existed was the misery of their confinement.

Men broke under this stress. They would announce that the next time they passed through the gate it would be on the dead wagon. Andrew McLean remembered that the cumulative effects of these conditions in the camp wore his fellow inmates down until they finally gave in and died. John Burton referred to the "plenty of sameness" and "tough times in old Georgia" in his diary. One soldier remembered how inmates would help anything green to grow in the stockade, even individual blades of grass, so as to encourage any life.

Many towns and regiments suffered from tragic statistical anomalies. None of the several prisoners from Pittsfield, New Hampshire, who entered Andersonville lived to see freedom. Teenager Michael Dougherty of the Thirteenth Pennsylvania Cavalry only barely survived sickness at Andersonville and the explosion of the troopship *Sultana* on his return home. The other 126 members of his regiment who entered Andersonville died in Southern captivity. James M. Emory of the Third Pennsylvania Heavy Artillery entered the camp with 15 comrades. Only he and one other of these men lived to leave. William O. Washburn entered the prison with almost 300 other members of the Sixteenth Indiana Cavalry. Of that number, 180 men died there, including 32 of the 53 men in his company. Everyone who survived from his Company M became seriously sick. Fourteen men survived the confinement only to later receive discharges as permanently disabled. Perry E. Carlton had 3 brothers held at Camp Sumter; 2 of his siblings died in Rebel captivity and 1 escaped. John Northrop wrote of 3 Tennessee brothers who, one by one, died in the same spot.

Tennesseans and other men from the states that officially seceded did draw special abuse from the guards and died at a corresponding rate. Confederate official H.A.M. Anderson even urged Captain Wirz to hold back from exchange any men who had deserted from the Southern army and joined the Federal service. When Confederate soldiers surrounded Colonel James P. Brownlow and his First Tennessee Cavalry (United States Army), he determined that he and his men would risk their lives trying to break out rather than become prisoners at Andersonville. He and his men succeeded in their escape. Prisoner poet John W. Northrop memorialized the service and sacrifice of the Tennesseans at Andersonville. Prisoner John McElroy would survive to write a prison novel that had Tennessee Unionists as the heroes. Deaths from their regiments propelled the Second Tennessee Infantry and the Seventh Tennessee Cavalry into the positions of having the third- and fourth-highest mortality rate, respectively, of any Federal units in Rebel captivity. They only ranked behind two New York regiments.

Other Southern Unionists, or "Tories," also especially suffered for their cause. Comparing the number of identified dead at Andersonville to the total number of men enlisted in the army by state, North Carolina has the worst mortality rate, followed by the Southern states of Tennessee, Alabama and Virginia/West Virginia, respectively. Robert H. Kellogg remembered the exceptional sufferings of white North Carolinians, or "buffaloes," as the guards called them, many of whom had previously deserted from the

Confederate army. He and his friends helped the men from the Second North Carolina Infantry hide their identities and unit from the guards. Of the thirty white men of the First Alabama Cavalry (U.S.A.) known to have found themselves in Andersonville, at least eighteen died there. The white Southerners were also attractive, because of their nativity, to Confederate recruiters, but few of them joined, or rejoined, the Confederate army.

Former Virginians (West Virginians after 1863) captured in Federal service also suffered terribly. Of the twenty men in Company I of the Tenth West Virginia who entered Andersonville, only Ransom T. Powell survived to go home. This thirteen-year-old boy believed that he lived only because a Confederate officer took pity on him and removed him from the inside of the stockade for use as a drummer boy.

Another group also received special notice. The guards placed black soldiers on work details that brought them extra physical labor and punishment but which, incidentally, allowed them better rations and thus a better chance at survival. Prisoner Reuben C. Griffitt believed that Southern fears of loss of social status by granting African Americans any rights at all and of violent slave revolts even extended to the guards at Camp Sumter. He felt that this inspired a particular hatred of Yankees that only increased toward black soldiers (many of whom had been slaves) and their white officers. Memoirists wrote of Confederate medical personnel denying attention to African American soldiers and their white officers. Rebel leaders sent the latter to Andersonville, despite their rank, rather than hang them, as prescribed by Confederate law, to block any exchange of the white officers of African soldiers. Planters came to the stockade to claim black soldiers as escaped slaves. Many of the white prisoners resented being imprisoned with black men or blamed African American soldiers for the breakdown in the prisoner exchange.

The inmates also suffered from a climate that was supposed to be so much milder than Virginia's. When lumber for prisoner housing finally arrived in early June, the guards appropriated it for their own use. The prisoners survived cold nights by huddling around any fire they could make, and during blazing hot days, they lived in holes in the ground. The walls of the stockade and the overcrowding blocked any breeze. Adding a space to keep prisoners away from the wall, called a dead line, and the swampy creek in the center of the stockade further reduced available space. An expansion of the prison on July 1 added more room, but at its height, the prison population barely had enough room for each man to lie down. The "fresh fish," or new prisoners, would become sick at first seeing the interior of the prison. Extra guards were needed, not just to force these newcomers into the stockade, but also to hold back the tens of thousands of prisoners who might have rushed out, if only for a brief moment in the fresh air.

Confederate Dr. Louis Manigault claimed that the situation at Andersonville was worse than anything he had seen in China. Sweetwater Creek, the sluggish stream that flowed through the center of the camp, became covered with insects and excrement. Efforts by Captain Wirz to have the water arranged by use—drinking, washing and sanitation—came to nothing when the prisoners stole the wood. Soldiers in need of drinking water would skim off the top of the creek to drink the water beneath it. Rain fell every day for an entire month in the summer of 1864, but these storms did not end the need for clean water. They did temporarily cover the stench that could be smelled for miles and the problem of lice, flies, mosquitoes and fleas. Maggots had also become so numerous that they made the ground appear to move. Many members of the garrison became sick from their duty at the prison, although, contrary to legend, they did not die at a rate anything near as high as that of the inmates.

The prisoners' clothes became rags, and many of their number were reduced to near nudity. The dead, sometimes more than one hundred per day, were stripped and left covered with only flies. Two slave-driven wagons, when filled with corn mush, served as the dispensary of rations to the prisoners, but they were also used for hauling out the dead. The camp cook, James W. Duncan, refused to allow the wagons to be washed out. For the first three hundred corpses, coffins were found; the nine hundred dead who followed them were covered by boards and boroughs. After that time, the dead received no more than space in trenches too shallow to deter vultures from preying on the bodies. Each deceased inmate received a numbered headboard and an often inaccurate or incomplete record of death.

Medical care also became a victim of greater government systems failure. The first hospital in the prison consisted of a single tent in the stockade. The camp administration later erected an enclosure for the sick outside of the stockade but next to a swamp and the sinks that were used as a latrine. Thousands of prisoners who needed medical attention had to lie on the ground, in the open air, with only what blankets they had. By the spring of 1865, after most of the prisoners had been transferred to other camps, sheds were built as a hospital. The need for a hospital still existed, for only the sickest prisoners had been left in the camp. Charges were made of incompetence and inefficiency against the prison's medical department. Prisoners who acted as nurses would also rob their patients and the hospital's stores. In his book defending the prison, Dr. R. Randolph Stevenson, director of the camp's hospital, failed to mention that he had been charged with embezzling $100,000 from his medical department.

The inmates created many of their own problems. Filthy habits of many of the men did not improve the situation. Gangs of desperate prisoners, many from the "Western swindlers" and the notorious street gangs of New York, robbed their fellow inmates. Entrepreneurs among their number grew rich trading between desperate prisoners and the guards, as well as from running gambling tents, at the expense of starving men. Inmates detailed to work outside of the stockade would steal from supplies reserved for the sick in the hospital and the camp bakery. Captain Wirz gave the prisoners tools with which to dig wells, only to have to withdraw them when the inmates used the opportunity to dig escape tunnels. His efforts to enclose the hospital against theft were also undone by the prisoners themselves.

Unintentionally, the Confederate government made matters even worse by creating three different independent chief administrative officers at Andersonville with no obligation to work together. The commandants of the prison commanded from the gate of the stockade to the area around Anderson Station. They were, in chronological order, Lieutenant Colonel Alexander W. Persons, Brigadier General John H. Winder and, finally, Colonel George Cooper Gibbs. Separately from the above, Lieutenant Colonel Alexander W. Persons, Colonel Edward O'Neal, Colonel James W. Fannin, Brigadier General Lucius Gartrell, Colonel Henry Forno and, lastly, Second Lieutenant Joel J. Easterlin commanded the troops assigned to guard the camp from prison breakouts and rescue attempts from outside. The stockade and its interior, as well as the guards on the wall, came to be the charge of Lieutenant Colonel Alexander William Persons until, in March 1864, Brigadier General Winder simultaneously assigned both Major Elias Griswold and Captain Henry Wirz to that responsibility before recalling Griswold. Persons then officially appointed Wirz to administer the interior of the stockade on March 29, 1864, more than a month after the prison opened. He thus unintentionally put Wirz on the road to being tried, found guilty and hanged by a United States military tribunal in the summer of 1865 for never-proven charges of cruelty and murder.

Initially, as shown above, Lieutenant Colonel Alexander William Persons of nearby Fort Valley, Houston County, and commander of what remained of the Fifty-fifth Georgia Infantry Regiment, originally held all three command positions at Andersonville simultaneously, although at least three officers present there outranked him. Officially, he was relieved of command in mid-June 1864 as part of a plan to solve the difficulties with Andersonville's organizational hierarchy by replacing him with Brigadier General John H. Winder, a plan that failed to sort out the greater problems of authority to find and obtain needed resources. He worked so tirelessly to find rations and other necessities for the camp that the prisoners believed that he was removed because he tried to help them. After he left, the lieutenant colonel did sue in court in an unsuccessful effort to close the prison as a public nuisance. He considered resigning his commission. A resident of Macon after the war, he died at Americus, near Andersonville, in May 1878.

Winder had complained that his authority did not extend beyond Richmond and that he had no responsibility for Andersonville. In June 1864, the Confederate government appointed him to the newly created position of the commander of all of the military prisons east of the Mississippi but then also ordered him to move from Richmond to Andersonville to concurrently serve as commandant of the prison. Under the general, the problems at Anderson Station grew worse, but not because he, in any way, conspired to harm anyone. He bluntly described the dire and deteriorating situation to superiors, who were only concerned with the security of Richmond and the Confederacy's failing war effort. What little time Winder spent at the prison made him sick. On December 31, 1864, he wrote to the Confederate secretary of war, in a private letter, about at least releasing the officers and the enlisted men whose time had run out, for reasons of internal security. Two days later, Winder appointed Brigadier General John B. Imboden commander of the prisons in Alabama, Georgia and Mississippi, an action that further confused the command situation.

Andersonville's command structure had many different problems. Officers tried to spend as much time as possible away from the prison and its many levels of horrors. Frequently, Wirz, who commanded no one and had frail health, found himself to be the highest-ranking officer at the prison and responsible for preventing a massive prisoner escape, despite the fact that he often found himself ignored by the camp's other administrators. The Confederate government in Richmond would sometimes, unintentionally, assign the same official position, simultaneously, to different officers at Andersonville who still could not issue orders beyond the camp. Major General Howell Cobb commanded the battalions of Georgia Reserves that guarded the prison, but he made his headquarters in Macon, Georgia. He answered to no one, including Winder, at Andersonville. The receipt of rations and medicines also depended on the actions of officers far from Anderson Station. In the prison, many critical jobs went to enlisted men, such as Private James W. Duncan, the cook for the tens of thousands of prisoners; Private Edward C. Turner, in charge of the packs of mongrels that had been trained to track slaves and now hunted the men imprisoned for joining an army sent to set slaves free; and seventeen-year-old Private Lemuel Madison Park, the commissary clerk. Even these men came from the Georgia state reserves and not the Confederate regular regiments.

The final horror for the inmates of the stockade at Andersonville was that, like some of the above guards, many of their numbers disappeared into the camp with no record of their arrivals and/or their fates. Many prisoners assumed the identities of dead prisoners or other men to obtain double rations. This idea worked with guards like William D. Hammock, who gave up trying to pronounce the names of his Yankees and simply counted heads at roll

This page and next: Life and death at Andersonville prison as remembered by former prisoner Thomas O'Dea. *Author's collection.*

call. Often, such men were added to the camp's incomplete rolls under their assumed names or as unknowns. One of the men eventually buried in the prison's cemetery, for example, used the identity of Ambrose Spencer of Company D of the Ninety-third New York Volunteers, although the real man of that name and unit survived the war. W.A. Jamieson successfully escaped from Andersonville, but on a visit to the site in 1916 he discovered that he had a tombstone in the prison's cemetery.

Many reasons exist for why a prisoner at Andersonville assumed a false identity. This prison quickly assumed such terrible notoriety that some men likely wanted their families to presume they had died in battle. Some prisoners assumed false identities to escape discovery, arrest and prosecution for crimes committed before reaching the prison. Felix DeLabaume of the Thirty-ninth New York, for example, would describe and even provide a drawing of conditions at the prison as evidence for Confederate captain Henry Wirz's postwar trial for war crimes. He became active in prisoner of war organizations after the war, despite being exposed as Ben Dykes of the Seventh New York, a deserter. A Dane called "Sandy" similarly made large sums of money from sales to desperate fellow prisoners. He had enlisted in and deserted the Federal army twice, however, before collecting still another enlistment bounty.

Some prisoners must have kept their new identities for the rest of their lives. Men have been using wars to escape from their pasts for as long as there have been armies. Other inmates left Andersonville with amnesia or other mental disorders. William "Crazy Jack" Newby of Tennessee and John B. Hotchkiss of New York drew national attention when they allegedly returned to their respective homes decades after the war. In Newby's case, he was so deranged that more than 140 different people saw him as who they wanted him to be. Newby's widow gave up her pension because she believed this man to be her husband, although more than 30 people swore that he was actually Daniel Benton of Tennessee and 6 other men swore that he was a demented prisoner at Andersonville called "Crazy Jack." The last record found of this man, whoever he may have been, would be a failed pension application that he filed from a poor farm near Andersonville in the late 1890s.

4

ESCAPING FROM ANDERSONVILLE

The inmates of Andersonville had every incentive to try to escape, and their sheer numbers so vastly outnumbered the resources of the guards that it seems the greatest mystery of the prison is that the men confined there did not just push down the wall and leave. Throughout the history of military prisons, however, the armed guards have always been greatly outnumbered by the inmates, yet prisoners almost never risk their lives in a mass breakout. What survives of the camp's records suggests that only about 1 in 230 men tried to escape from Andersonville.

Even within that limited subgroup, many of the prisoners only sought to escape in order to find green leaves and weeds to eat or to get away, at least briefly, from the almost overwhelming stench and swarms of insects. John Northrop wrote of men getting out of the stockade, spending a few days being fed and hidden by slaves and then giving themselves up to the nearest authorities. John Ransom worked for months with his friends on a tunnel. When he finally escaped, however, he only hoped that he would reach a house and food before the guards returned him to the prison and punishment on a chain gang in the stockade. After his recapture, he discovered that he received better treatment and more rations while on the camp's punishment detail. Prisoner Robert Sneden wrote that fewer than one in twenty of the inmates who volunteered to work on building the camp cookhouse knew anything about carpentry or bricklaying. They lied just for the chance to leave the stockade and to get extra rations.

Trees that marked the escape tunnels at Andersonville. *Courtesy of Georgia Archives, Vanishing Georgia Collection, Sum105.*

An occasional show of force, such as parading the troops, calling out the local militia or firing a cannon or two reinforced the perceived threat of the garrison's ability to kill at least some inmates during a mass escape. The post commanders, such as Lieutenant Colonel Persons, seemed to understand that they retained power only through the threat of violence. They dared not actually use it to force the prisoners to make the decision of choosing to join a breakout or simply dying. The garrison would ignore Captain Henry Wirz's pleas to fire on the prisoners, such as when a riot broke out during the hanging of bandit leaders by the inmates.

The threat of the use of mass violence deters group escape attempts, but isolation also makes for a strong prison. Such camps are often built so far behind the lines that any group that escapes has to traverse great distances of hostile territory and then pass through the enemy army. Getting to Andersonville, for example, required a train ride of hundreds of miles through a seemingly uninhabited forest. This journey not only discouraged escape but also implanted in the prisoners the idea of a

Confederate States of America too big to conquer. A man could escape from the prison, guards, dogs, militia, slave patrols, posses, armed civilians, bears and everything else with no idea about what to do next. Camp stories about using tree moss, watercourses, the sun, etc., for direction often proved inaccurate. Henry M. Davidson of the First Ohio Light Artillery and his two comrades had a printed map, a compass and careful planning. They successfully evaded dogs and guards only to run into capture by the Confederate army while only a short distance from Sherman's lines. Tired and hungry escapees would turn themselves in after having been out for weeks. Starting in September 1864, large groups of prisoners left Andersonville almost unhindered in an effort to reach the Federal armies around Atlanta. By then, however, militias and state guards had been embodied across Georgia. They arrested the escapees and sent them on to the horrors of the last Confederate prisons.

The other great psychological barrier used to keep prisoners imprisoned involved potential release. Andersonville's administration encouraged rumors that exchanges were or would soon be negotiated; the prisoners only had to wait patiently for release. Sumter County's newspaper reprinted any story about a pending exchange. Specific groups—such as sailors, Sherman's cavalrymen and the sickest prisoners—would be exchanged. This encouraged hope among the men left behind. News reports of the success of the advancing Federal forces were kept from the prisoners with limited success. The guards on the wall, for example, called out the news on the night that Atlanta fell to Sherman.

According to legend, no one successfully escaped from the prison. Prison memoirists estimated that somewhere between one (DeLayvan Streeter) and twenty-five men made successful runs to freedom. Scattered memoirs and newspaper reports support the latter number, although defining escape can be difficult, as many prisoners counted merely surviving the prison as escape. No large group of inmates found their way to freedom, but small parties of three or four members could succeed. Daring escapes happened more in legend than in reality.

Newspaper accounts and prisoner memoirs imply a great deal about the select group of men who at least tried to escape. Length of time in captivity meant nothing. Men who escaped together in small groups seldom came from the same regiment or even the same state. They seem to have come together chiefly out of a deep-seated need to escape and acted out of opportunity rather than desperation. Most men who tried to escape would do so repeatedly and often. Even after escaping from the Confederacy, they would continue to escape for the rest of their lives.

What records that survive fail to answer the question of just how many men succeeded in escaping from Andersonville. Camp Sumter (Andersonville) opened in late February 1864, but its morning reports begin on April 1, when Captain Henry Wirz assumed charge of the prisoners. On that date, the stockade held 7,106 prisoners, and the cemetery held 304 more. Over the rest of the prison's history, the records show 328 escapes from the camp, a tiny fraction of the total 2,696 men estimated to have escaped from the Confederacy as a whole. The morning reports also show that 181 men were recaptured and brought back to Andersonville, although men who escaped from prison trains going to or from the camp were counted. Prisoners not in those statistics included men who were retaken late in the war and then went to the prisons established after Andersonville had been reduced to more of a hospital than a prison. No way of counting the men who died from starvation and exposure in the vast, empty wilderness of the Deep South exists.

Some men would get out of the stockade more than once and would sometimes be counted as two or more escapes and recaptures. Henry Clay Hartwell made two escapes and tried another, all without success. On his last effort, he and his partners went to the new Camp Lawton Prison at Millen, Georgia, and were not reported at Andersonville as recaptured.

The prisoners were caught between hope of imminent release and dying before they could be released. Escape became the third option. Henry Clay Damon of the Eleventh Michigan Infantry Regiment, one of the few men to successfully escape from the prison, reported that the comrades he had left behind had concealed three hundred pistols, although he may have meant only three handguns. On April 20, an informant exposed a plot of the inmates to tunnel out, take the guards and use civilians as hostages. The local militia came out to help deter this scheme. Captain Wirz exposed a plot by the inmates to undermine the stockade and seize the prison's artillery before disarming the guards and fleeing to Pensacola. Federal officers at Camp Oglethorpe in Macon plotted to tunnel out and release the prisoners at Andersonville. They would have carried out this scheme by disarming their guards, seizing additional weapons at the Macon Arsenal and stealing a train. As usual, they were betrayed.

As the Confederate cause became obviously lost and the notoriety of Andersonville spread, more and more people helped escaped prisoners. A desperate fugitive would risk arrest, even by housewives and children, when approaching a farmhouse, but he could also find help, such as what John R. Tate received from a small boy, Z.T. Walker, and the child's brother and sister some six miles from Andersonville. The children's neighbor, Mrs. Cunningham, also often fed escapees, but she did so out of fear. Agnes Spencer of Sumter County and Emily Karnes of Talbot County, among others, hid prisoners and nursed them back to health. An unknown soldier from Lexington, Kentucky, received aid from Spencer. He had fled on a freezing cold day in January 1865, apparently without further thought about how he would escape. Recaptured, he made a rare escape directly from the guards. With only rags for clothes, he hid in winter weather for three days before a sympathetic slave found him and directed him to the Spencer home. Agnes fed, clothed and sheltered the fugitive until he could safely move on to rescue at St. Marks, Florida. The soldier had lived so primitively for so long that he had to relearn how to use eating utensils. Charles Mather Smith, Dr. Ashley W. Barrows and Allington A. Crandall escaped to Florida, where they reached a passing Federal ship thanks to help from the father of four dead Confederate soldiers, a frightened Unionist and a one-armed pirate. Escaped prisoners also discovered that whole communities of fugitive white Southerners, escaped slaves and deserters from both armies had come into being in the mountains and swamps, such as the secret refugee settlement of Devil's Swamp, North Carolina.

According to legend, Civil War prison escapes were most often made by tunnels. So much of this kind of work went on at Andersonville that the railroad siding of Anderson Station became a mining boomtown, with freedom the great treasure being obtained from the earth. Prisoners, or "shareholders," did form "mining companies" of some one hundred men to excavate secret passages under the palisades, but as events proved, this was more as recreation than as a practical means of achieving freedom. Captain Henry Wirz reported that from when he started keeping records on April 1, 1864, to the end of July, eighty-three excavations had been found and filled. One member of the garrison would even attribute the creation of the Providence Spring, the source of badly needed fresh water in the stockade that reportedly came about from a lightning bolt, to depressions caused by so many tunnels.

Discounting rumors and exaggerations, it may actually have been that as few as only one digger may have succeeded in getting out of the stockade. Diaries confirm that wild stories flew about the camp, exaggerating the number of men who escaped. Few, if any, of these inmates succeeded in escaping to the Federal lines. Making such an escape attempt proved problematic. Diggers had to make tools from whatever they could find, such as halved canteens for shovels and bootlegs as buckets. Entrances to tunnels were disguised with wells, shelters, blankets, trash and sick soldiers. Various means had to be devised for scattering dirt around the stockade undetected by the guards. Advice would be sought from participants in earlier projects, even from men who had failed, and inmates would leave one scheme for another, depending on progress. The need for air limited a project to a tunnel that could extend only from ten to five hundred feet long and some twenty feet underground. A tunnel had to go down at least eight feet and then run horizontally at least thirty feet to clear the camp's palisade and the dead line.

Warren Goss helped to dig two tunnels that failed to even cross the dead line. In his second attempt, he owed his rescue, from a cave-in, to the guards. Homemade means to keep the digging level and heading toward the outside sometimes failed, and the prisoners could find themselves digging short of the wall. John McElroy and his "company" dug a tunnel for forty feet before it collapsed inside the camp. They had lost their direction and had unintentionally dug in a horseshoe shape that brought the end of the tunnel back to within fifteen feet of where it had begun. Discovery of excavations occurred by many means. The weight of the palisades sometimes caused the logs to crash through the tunnel ceilings. Sometimes the guards would be able to save the digger.

Timing also would prove critical, as the final push would need to be in the dark, when rain would protect them from being followed by dogs or when Georgia's notoriously noisy summer insects could hide their noise. Predicting exactly when a tunnel would clear the stockade proved impossible. Reuben Griffitt became a "stockholder" in several of these ventures, although he never escaped by tunnel. He found that the final push out could take forty-eight hours, forty-eight minutes or a week.

Too many obstacles stood in the way of a successful tunnel. Seemingly as fast as an excavation began, paid informants, or "tunnel traitors," reported the new project to Captain Wirz. Allegedly, an individual reward might be as small as a plug of tobacco that a desperate prisoner could trade for food. Thomas W. "Chickamauga" Hurlbut was the one-legged soldier famously ordered shot by a guard on May 16, 1864, after he had fled into the dead line space, despite warnings, while running from a mob of prisoners who believed he had reported on their tunnel. Captain Wirz would even disguise guards as prisoners to uncover plots to escape. Guards watched for suspicious activities from the pigeon roosts. An effort to leave this "Eve-less Eden" by the ever-sarcastic Charles Richardson of the Seventy-sixth New York ended when a guard caught him discharging dirt hidden in his shirt. In one instance, five hundred men were reportedly caught when they were seen around a hole, waiting for a chance to escape.

The guards played many roles in their game of defeating escape by tunnel. Slave workers were made to use crowbars to probe the ground for tunnels. In late July, prison officials ringed the prison with a second stockade, two hundred feet outside of the original wall, and began construction on a third wall, in part to require diggers to extend their work even farther to reach the outside. The guards finally detailed prisoners to add a trench inside the dead line to expose any tunnels. By August 23, 1864, as the opportunity to escape to Sherman's army near Atlanta seemed like an increasing possibility, a nightly picket line of guards around the camp increased the possibility of detection.

Tunnels did prove a source of entertainment for the whole prison, raising morale, but they also provided false hopes that discouraged the inmates from the more practical solution of organizing a mass rush on the poorly armed and badly outnumbered guards. The obvious lack of success of the tunnels suggests that the prisoners worked on them more as an act of defiance and even recreation than out of any realistic hope of getting out of the stockade. It became almost their only form of amusement, other than gambling or prayer/patriotic meetings, in the overcrowded prison. (Inmates detailed to live and work outside of the stockade, however, played baseball and even socialized with the few local civilians.)

The tunnel projects also became great sources for stories. John North-rop of the Seventy-sixth New York wrote in his diary of one hapless digger coming up beneath an armed guard. Another group of diggers reportedly broke into a tent where two of the guards were playing cards. On another occasion, a digger came up underneath a guard sleeping on the ground. One night, a tunnel project ended up on a small hill underneath a campfire where some of the Georgia Reserves were sleeping or warming themselves. The guards fled in terror. Inmates in Andersonville were "smoked"; that is, covered in soot from the softwood campfire smoke that drifted across the camp. The superstitious Southerners mistook the first man out of the tunnel for the devil rising from hell! The first digger escaped, although the guards soon had his partners in custody.

Some men did, at least according to legend, succeed in getting out. William L. Farmer of the 111th Illinois Volunteers even used the shortcomings of the tunnels to escape. A prisoner at Andersonville for only two weeks after his capture on June 8, 1864, he blackmailed some diggers into allowing him to join them by threatening to report their tunnel to the Confederates. When a man working on the excavation failed to return one night, Farmer drew the lot to crawl in and see if the digger had escaped or had become trapped in a cave-in. Farmer discovered that the digger had made it out and escaped. Instead of reporting back to his partners, he, too, took the opportunity to flee. He hid in the swamps a quarter of a mile from the prison, using the water to shield his scent from the hounds. Slaves concealed and fed him until he could reach the Federal lines.

Most escapes actually began with the prisoner fleeing from one of the camp's various work details. In his June 1864 returns, for example, Captain Henry Wirz wrote that all of that month's escapees had fled from work details. The volunteers on this duty faced scorn, and sometimes physical abuse, from men who remained inside the stockade and saw these volunteer workers as collaborators and traitors. In addition to the guarded groups of workmen needed to bring in wood and take out the dead, Wirz often had at least three hundred Yankees working outside the walls on parole. He had to continue allowing them to live outside the stockade, even after a group of them assaulted his family and took Wirz's buggy for a joy ride.

Punishments for such transactions and escapes usually only lasted a few hours. Inmate Herman A. Braun believed that the guards only punished those prisoners of war who had violated oaths by trying to escape while on duty outside of the prison, although Pennsylvania cavalryman Aaron Bachman claimed that even under those circumstances the punishments could prove fatal. Bachman heard of a group of prisoners who enlisted in the Confederate army and, after mutinying, killed two officers and took the rest of the unit as hostages. Supposedly, sick men they had to leave behind suffered execution in retaliation for the two dead Confederate soldiers. He also claimed that a dozen well-fed men from the cookhouse work detail obtained pistols and killed the dogs that pursued them in their escape. After their recapture, Bachman remembered that he watched as, starved and chained together day after day, all but three of the men died.

The first officially noted escapes, in April 1864, proved typical in that the men fled work details. Three men tried to escape on April 15 (names and circumstances unknown), but they had been captured by the next roll call. More than a week later, an inmate fled from the hospital, where he worked as an attendant, but the guards brought him back in less than twenty-four hours. Three men, soon after, jumped a guard while on a wood detail and ran into the woods. The dogs soon tracked them down. A short time later, three more inmates made the same attempt. The guards brought back two men and believed that the third prisoner of war had drowned. They were mistaken. Tom Williams, the other man, survived to reach the Federal lines and then later suffer capture again.

In August, eleven men left work gangs after giving oaths that they would not try to escape. Frank Maddox, aka Mattock, of the Thirty-fifth United States Colored Troops (formerly the First North Carolina Colored Infantry) witnessed a disguised white prisoner named Bardo caught and punished for trying to leave the camp on a work detail of black prisoners. Prisoners Jasper Culver and Lewis Trowbridge made bread at the camp's bakery and loaded the dead/ration wagons, giving them access not only to the outside of the stockade but also to rations to take with them during their escape. Private Sidney Moore of the Fifteenth New York Infantry made an escape from the camp bakery and, aided by slaves, traveled north to rescue by McCook's cavalry near Atlanta. Dr. Ashley W. Barrows of the Twenty-seventh Massachusetts fled the camp's hospital, where he worked as a doctor. The majority of the members of a burial detail took off on September 8.

Bribes to guards could facilitate such escapes. Michael Dougherty of the 30th Pennsylvania Cavalry wrote that prisoners used work details as opportunities for illicit trade for food with the guards, thereby creating contacts in the garrison. Captain Wirz claimed that of the thirty men who left in August, of whom the guards had caught six, all had bribed guards with Federal currency or ran off from work details. William Ray Toney, Roe Asburn and a third man effectively used a twenty-dollar gold piece to persuade a guard to look the other way and let them flee. Sergeant George H. Fonner of the 101st Pennsylvania made a typical escape. He bribed a guard to allow him to flee from the hospital detail. Fonner reached Federal forces near Atlanta hiding under sacks of corn in a slave-driven wagon headed to the Confederate army. For the fact that the garrison failed to capture such fugitives, Wirz blamed the guards, who avoided reporting the men as escaped. Usually, only during morning roll call were the escapees missed.

Beyond tunnels and escaping from work details, prisoner M.V.B. Phillips remembered that the variety of means of escape attempts were numerous, odd and "frequently amusing." He wrote of the bean box escape whereby prisoners left the stockade by hiding in the crates on the wagon that had brought in the prisoner's rations. Robert Knox Sneden remembered four or five prisoners escaping by that means on September 7, 1864. John McElroy wrote of a prisoner caught trying to leave the stockade by hanging on to the bottom of the ration wagon. J.N. Hall of the 113th Ohio and a soldier named Williams escaped, in the dark, by passing through where the camp's creek flowed out of the stockade. The dog pack caught Hall, but he believed that his friend got away. Frederick Guscetti of the 47th New York attempted to leave by posing as a corpse; as on some days more than one hundred men died in the prison, hiding among the bodies did not pose a problem. Several prisoners left by that means until informants exposed this trick to the guards. Striped almost naked, Guscetti thus rode out of the stockade on the same two-mule wagon that brought in rations. Captain Wirz discovered him outside, however, but pitying the prisoner, he ordered clothes for him and his return to the stockade unpunished. Another soldier, trying to leave by this means, almost escaped. His "rising" from the dead frightened and alarmed his black teamster, who then alerted the guard. An Ohio soldier did get out of Andersonville with the daily piles of dead through the help of his friends. He nearly surrendered when one of his friends tried to "help" him by suggesting to the guards that they shoot the "corpse" as insurance.

Other prisoners tried to directly violate the stockade's walls. Men could slip undetected through gaps during autumn fogs. C.A. Smith of the Eleventh Iowa remembered four men, on a dark night, reaching the stockade and simply digging directly under it. They escaped, but with the help of the dog pack, the guards brought them back the next day. Smith sarcastically wrote that the guards tried to protect the prisoners from becoming lost in the swamps and falling prey to some beast. When rains caused a part of the stockade to fall, the camp authorities had it shored up with crossbeams nailed to the interior of the wall. William Burge of the Eleventh Iowa took advantage of the repairs to climb the wall on a dark, stormy night. Despite the rain and having to cross the Flint River, the dogs still tracked him down. The pack handler treated him kindly, and even Captain Wirz only punished him with a large dose of the captain's famous profanity. John McElroy of the Sixteenth Illinois Cavalry, and fifty other prisoners, tried to leave the stockade in the dark by climbing over the wall with a rope. The guards, warned by an informant, allowed fifteen men to get over. As each prisoner scaled the wall, the guards silently held a gun to his head and led him away to punishment on the chain gang.

Other prisoners simply walked out of the stockade. George W. Rumble of the Third New York Cavalry made up enough of a Confederate uniform to blend in with the guards and then left with a train load of conscripts heading to the front, from where he escaped to the Federal lines. Similarly, Henry Clay Damon of the Eleventh Michigan and William Smith of the Fourteenth Pennsylvania Cavalry traded for gray garments worn by Tennessee Federal soldiers. The Confederates who had originally captured the Tennesseans made them exchange their uniforms for the gray rags their captors wore. When sergeants came in to take roll as usual, the two Yankees slipped out with them, disguised as sergeants. Damon even completed his disguise by carrying what looked like a roll book. They then continued their journey until reaching the Union army in Tennessee. During their twenty-three-day journey, they did not encounter any Confederate soldiers.

By means of contrast, Private Lawrence LeBron of the Eleventh Illinois would claim that he fought his way to freedom, in early September 1864, without anyone's help. He wrote that the Confederates included him in a party of prisoners shipped to another prison camp. He feigned illness and held back until he and his guard were alone. He pretended to need to relieve himself, and he and his guard stopped. LeBron then allegedly killed the soldier, took the dead man's musket and clothes and dumped the body over a bridge. Reaching the train at dusk, LeBron rode atop a car, where he pretended to be a guard. Some twenty miles from Andersonville, he jumped from the train. Defying mosquitoes, heat, snakes, hostile Southerners of both races and alligators, he reached north Georgia and, almost, Sherman's armies. He then avoided Davidson's mistake of trying to pass through the Confederate army. Instead, he used stars to steer him west to Mississippi. After two months of hiding and dodging, he finally returned to Federal lines, close to where he had been captured while working as a scout a year earlier.

Several inmates escaped by using ruses to join in prisoner exchanges, what the prisoners referred to as "flanking out." Some men bribed guards for places on those train rides home. The notorious gamblers Charles Ellis and George W. Fechter, as well as J.C. Tarsney (pretending to be the dead John Fultz), left that way. William Batterton of the 114th Illinois and others fell in with men chosen for an exchange and so escaped. Jasper Culver and two other prisoners did the same but later fell out of the group and hid in the bushes before they could be caught boarding the train without authorization. When the doctors selected sick soldiers for return to the Federal lines, the Confederate surgeons passed over Private Passmore W. Hoopes of the 1st Pennsylvania Reserve Infantry. Returning to the stockade, he believed that he would die in the prison. With inspiration born of desperation, he ran to his "shebang" (hovel) and grabbed

This page and next: Escape, capture and punishment were popular themes in prisoner memoirs and illustrations, although almost all escapes were made by fleeing from work details and not by tunnels. *Author's collection.*

his haversack. Returning to the gate, he told the guards that the surgeons had selected him for the return to the Federal lines and that he had only gone back for his belongings. Always pictured as gullible in these stories, the sentries ordered him to hurry along as the train started to pull out. Hoopes thus caught his ride to freedom. When sailors received an exchange, Sergeant Hiram Buckingham of the 16th Connecticut Infantry obtained enough of a navy uniform to pass out of the prison by assuming the identity of dead sailor Johnny Sullivan. Prison officials recorded his escape without ever learning how he left.

Federal records credit David Jones, David Hughes and David Winn (David Weir?), all of Pennsylvania regiments and probably in the same mess, along with scout Thomas Cheshire of Tennessee, with making the greatest of these escapes when figured in miles. The Federal commissary general of prisoners listed them as traveling more than two thousand miles from Andersonville to Key West, Florida. A newspaper account, however, sets the record straight. They bribed a guard to let them escape when they went out one night. Upon leaving Andersonville, they fled through swamps until they found a sympathetic slave. Their new friend carried them in his wagon, under a load of corn, for seventy miles through two towns and across a ferry. Another slave guided them to white Floridians who supported the Union. These allies gave the fugitives a boat on Ochlockonee Bay, near Tallahassee. The United States mortar schooner *Oliver H. Lee*, en route to Key West, finally rescued the fugitives. These escapees did suffer hardships, including having only raw sweet potatoes to eat, but they only traveled some two hundred miles while on the run.

Union soldiers came to the South for a cause that, in time, came to include freeing the slaves. The African Americans they came to liberate, however, proved to be the greatest allies to escaping prisoners. The same network that had helped slaves reach the North now helped these Federal soldiers safely reach the Union lines. *Author's collection.*

Plantation owners helped their workers evade being taken into the cause of maintaining slavery. Without any connection to the prewar Underground Railroad, the risks that these African Americans took in helping fugitive Yankees likely began out of pity, which only some of their white neighbors shared.

The Andersonville survivors failed to see the irony of their situation, but Winslow Homer captured it in an unnamed painting, composed between 1865 and 1866, that has since popularly come to be known as *Near Andersonville*. He painted a slave woman watching Federal prisoners being escorted back to the prison after a failed escape attempt. She wears a turban—a rite of passage that demonstrated her maturity and ability to handle responsibility. Watching the captured Yankees marked a moment in her own transition from slave to free. When emancipation came, many of her friends and family, perhaps she as well, would wear hats as a symbol of self-determination. To black abolitionist Sojourner Truth, this painting showed how the sufferings of the Yankee prisoners at Andersonville became one of the many ways that America would pay for allowing slavery. In another interpretation, the painting represents how white Northerners helped slaves to escape through the "free states" of the North to Canada along the Underground Railroad.

Now African Americans helped fugitive white men escape Southern confinement, white men who had been sent south to end black slavery.

Fear of conspiracies among the enslaved became one of the great common threads of the history of slavery in Georgia, and as early as 1844, a white Georgian reported how the state's workers in bondage readily believed that "great men" would soon set them free. Statistics from the slave schedules of the 1850 census, however, show that few black Americans successfully escaped. The 1860 schedule shows that even fewer of them made that journey successfully following the Fugitive Slave Act of 1850. Anecdotal evidence shows that such fugitives more likely found themselves recaptured, kidnapped, returned to masters and/or sold to new owners, even when legally free. Some rebellions did occur. For example, some slaves escaped to form communities in the swamps of Florida and, in the decade before the Civil War, defeated all attempts to recapture them. What few records exist of pre–Civil War escapes omit any mention of Macon and Sumter Counties.

These attempts to escape helped bring on the Civil War and eventually turned that conflict into a war of liberation. Except for the rare and isolated slave revolt, the Underground Railroad and escape attempts represented the principal oppositions to slavery. Escape, like sabotage and work slowdowns, became part of a popular alternative campaign to bring down the institution of slavery by slaves who chose not to take up the suicidal course of armed confrontation against their masters. This other war depended on individuals rather than on an organized conspiracy. Without membership in organizations, escapees avoided betrayal and the inciting of widespread and violent white retaliation. As their descendants would do in the 1960s, by avoiding their own use of violence, the runaway slaves also spared their white sympathizers from having to condone threats to life and property, even in a noble cause. Many more slaves helped others to escape than tried to escape themselves.

Helping prisoners of the Confederacy to reach Federal lines must have seemed a natural extension of these tactics. Slaves in southwest Georgia, even though they were far beyond the reach of the famous Underground Railroad and born in imprisonment, had well learned the problems of escaping by the time of the Civil War. By the winter of 1864, patrols for escaped slaves had also become ineffective. The slaves now regarded themselves as all but self-emancipated. Some of them joined the some 500,000 slaves who escaped to the Federal lines; 19,000 of them would join Sherman's march across Georgia. These freedom fighters provided the Union army with information, workers and distractions for the Confederacy's declining military and, ultimately, solders and sailors.

They also felt that they could help Yankee prisoners, despite rumors that the Confederates had spies disguised as escaped soldiers. While a great deal has appeared in print about slaves as soldiers, and to a lesser extent as refugees, almost nothing has been published about them as conductors of their own underground railroad for fugitive white men. Some prison writers would later emphasize the aid provided by slaves to educate the public that emancipation had also been an effort by the enslaved to free themselves, not just an abstract Yankee social ideal imposed on all races and classes of the South by Federal force and blood. These prisoner narratives omit any portrayal of African Americans as stupid, childish or naïve, despite similar negative descriptions of poor Southern whites. Writers of the escape memoirs remembered the slave families as always striving to stay together, even when members lived on different plantations—an important observation often missed by many of the owners. Medal of Honor winner and Andersonville survivor David F. Day would provide free advertising for his local African Methodist church, which responded by making him its one white member. He also provided Thanksgiving dinner each year for his African American acquaintances because of the aid given to him by slaves when he escaped from Andersonville and Florence Prisons.

Unfortunately, the records remain silent on the names of the slaves who dared to help the white fugitives of Andersonville. Almost every credible account of escape from the prison mentions the help of African Americans. In 1948, E. Merton Coulter even made the comment, in describing the published memoirs of Henry M. Davidson, that it "is surprisingly free from hackneyed stories of heroic slaves assisting prisoners of war to escape." Coulter's opinion aside, Davidson wrote his book to push for an exchange of prisoners and likely omitted references to the slaves in order to avoid hurting his cause by aggravating already inflamed racial prejudices among his white readers in the North.

The account of Thomas Hinds, native Irishman and teenage member of the First Maryland Infantry, best illustrates the help frequently received from blacks during an escape from Anderson Station. He had already learned that he could get aid from slaves during a previous unsuccessful attempt to flee near Macon. Hinds left Andersonville on the pretense of being part of a detail to gather wood for a shelter on June 6, 1864. To facilitate his escape, he waited until he had a fat, elderly conscript from Mobile, of known good nature, as his only guard. When the sentry looked in another direction, Hinds quietly slipped into the woods and escaped. The rain from a sudden thunderstorm masked his scent from pursuing dogs.

Along his route, slave families often helped him. At different times, they provided him with food, clothes, shoes, money, a gun, a knife, medical attention and even a map from an atlas. One of their number carried the escaped Yankee some distance to conceal Hinds's scent from dogs. His benefactors even tried to fit him in a dress to disguise him as a slave girl. Hinds needed their help, for he had left the prison with no real idea about what to do next. For much of his odyssey, he had a recurring fever and painful, swollen feet.

During his journey, he learned much about slavery in the Old South. On a Dr. Winn's plantation, he discovered that several of the slaves had learned to read, a rarity among that population. A black blacksmith took him to the plantation prayer meetings. Hinds met a native African and also an elderly man who had lived throughout Georgia and had tried to escape several times. The two veteran fugitives likely shared experiences. A black overseer betrayed Hinds near Butler, Georgia, resulting in his capture on June 14 by a posse of old men and boys armed with a motley assortment of weapons. A Confederate officer, home on medical furlough, talked his neighbors out of hanging the Yankee soldier as a professional courtesy. Instead, they displayed him to the local women before carrying him to jail in Butler. While later in prison in Macon, he overpowered the keeper, who died from a resulting heart attack, and fled in the rain. While still in the yard, Hinds accidentally knocked down a black female servant and only barely avoided entanglement in a clothesline. Near the jail, he quietly blended into a crowd of fifteen hundred to two thousand people who had gathered around the train depot to welcome Brigadier General John H. Winder as he changed trains en route to his duties at Andersonville.

Slave and free families continued to help Hinds. Near Stone Mountain, a slave took him to a Unionist white overseer who worked for a Mr. Graham of Kentucky, a former schoolmate of Abraham Lincoln. Ironically, Hinds soon after displayed incredible ingratitude when he declined to join forty slaves in trying to reach the Federal lines for fear of recapture and execution. In July, he finally reached the Federal army with the help of a large family of poor white millworkers at Roswell. Unbeknownst to Hinds, General Sherman almost certainly included this family among the civilians he ordered to the North to end their use as skilled workers by the Confederacy. As with almost all of these special prisoners, they likely never acquired the means to return home to Georgia.

Of the one hundred or more African American soldier inmates at Andersonville, at least one of them, Richard Holmes of Lawrence County, Alabama, a member of the 106th United States Colored Troops, escaped. His records fail to mention how he did it. Holmes had a special disadvantage in that Southern slave patrols had dogs specifically trained to follow persons of African descent. No one offered black soldiers the chance to leave Andersonville by enlisting in the Confederate army.

Curiously, a few prisoners benefited from, and some of them even achieved release from Andersonville for, failing in their escape attempts. Jim Mallory supposedly reached the Federal lines several times, only to find himself back in Andersonville each time. James R. Compton credited this constant "misfortune" to Mallory being a spy who passed back and forth to the prison with information. Robert H. Kellogg saw four men rewarded with double rations out of admiration for their tunnel after the guards found and stopped their excavation. At Wirz's trial, the prosecution claimed that the camp dogs attacked a Canadian prisoner named Frado (popularly known as "Little Frenchy"), who later died in the stocks. Wirz and his witnesses, however, claimed that the dogs did not harm the prisoner and that Frado even laughed at the canines. Little Frenchy, in fact, escaped at least seven times, including once by tunnel and once while on his way to the camp's blacksmith for shackling to the chain gang. On one occasion, even while chained, he escaped. Chains, stocks and other punishments proved ineffective in containing this man's exceptional case of barbed wire disease.

To discourage Frado's escapes, Wirz claimed that he paroled Frado to live and work outside of the stockade, action that would have rewarded the prisoner with extra rations. Little Frenchy, however, refused to do physical labor and continued to try to escape. Local people, using dog packs, kept bringing him back, except when he gave up and returned voluntarily. Captain Wirz finally sent him out for exchange, but even on his way home, Frado reportedly escaped again, this time while passing through Macon. He survived to receive exchange in Annapolis, Maryland.

Sergeant Leroy L. Key of the Sixteenth Illinois Cavalry had an equally interesting experience in earning his exchange. After helping to suppress the prison's bandits, he received a job as a cook outside of the stockade to protect him from the friends of the thieves. When he heard of the pending exchange of his squad, he pleaded to go with them. Captain Wirz, however, refused to allow the kitchen help to leave Andersonville until everyone else had received release. Key and four other men escaped. The prison's dogs ran past their hiding place without finding them. The fugitives then traveled eight days before civilians apprehended them. Their captors refused to accept bribes to let them go and took them to the jail in Hamilton. The local women did provide them with a fine meal, however. Confederate authorities transferred Key to Macon, where, on five different occasions, Key faked being sick to avoid transfer to a prison camp. He tried, unsuccessfully, to escape before he really did become sick and, fortuitously, again missed the train to prison. The Confederate officials finally included him in a special exchange of ill prisoners.

Other men did worse than just fail in an attempt to escape from Camp Sumter, and some of them had adventures that rivaled those of the fictional Arly and Will in E.L. Doctorow's novel *The March*. They failed repeatedly, despite their best efforts. Cassius M. Ellis of the Sixty-fourth New York Infantry became a guest of the Confederate States of America on three separate occasions, in battle at Fair Oaks, Gettysburg and Petersburg, respectively. He reached freedom once by exchange and twice by escape. While at Andersonville, he witnessed his brother's death. After he escaped from Camp Sumter, Cassius traveled two hundred miles and spent a month in a South Carolina swamp before finding rescue on the coast.

John Burke tried to escape from Andersonville three times, once from a work detail, once in a tunnel and once while left alone at a burial. In his first escape, his recapture took place in a nearby barn. On his second try, a traitor exposed the tunnel, and the guards captured him and his friends as they came out. Finally, he suffered arrest by three boys and a disabled soldier. He survived the punishment detail each time.

Similarly, William P. Reed, an alumnus of the Cahawba Prison, came within forty miles of the safety of Pensacola before dogs tracked him down and their handlers took him back, in chains, to Andersonville. Later, he tried to float to freedom on a log before a slave betrayed him. While on parole in Savannah, he escaped again and lived by begging before a Unionist family took him in. Once again, he suffered recapture. Reed finally jumped from a train to reach freedom.

Samuel Griswold, an unarmed Jones County boy, peacefully captured such an Andersonville escapee near his home. The unlucky soldier had made two other unsuccessful escape attempts. He bitterly complained that the Federal government refused to exchange him because his enlistment had run out. The army preferred to exchange Confederates for soldiers with time left on their enlistments rather than for men who would be released to return home. The sympathetic Griswolds provided him with a meal, a bath and a sack of food before sending him back to Andersonville.

Other prisoners had equally unfortunate experiences. Hugh R. Snee and another inmate jumped the boy guarding them on a work detail but succeeded in fleeing only far enough to suffer recapture by the mounted patrol that circled the camp. Shortly afterward, Snee and other prisoners, while being transferred to another prison, suffered a train wreck. Snee found himself returned to Andersonville but with severe wounds that went untreated by the prison staff. The unfortunate soldier later tried to leave the camp with the men sent to Sherman's army for exchange, by posing as a prisoner from Sherman's command that he heard had died. The dead man's friends, however, stopped him because they had decided to use this ruse with someone else. Snee later tried to join the men for the exchange anyway. He took advantage of the confusion in the roll call to act as someone marked for release. From then until Snee slipped out and walked the last few miles to Sherman's lines, he had to hide each time the guards called roll.

Hiram S. Daskam of the Third Iowa Infantry succeeded in sneaking out of the prison with a group of inmates who believed they had earned exchange. The camp authorities had lied to them. The train they boarded began their journey to the new prison pen at Florence, South Carolina. He and many other men jumped from the train when they learned the truth. Daskam suffered recapture within a few miles of the Federal lines in coastal North Carolina. He only reached safety, near Knoxville, Tennessee, after two more escape attempts.

Particularly cruel twists of fate awaited the men who tried to escape the days of the Confederacy's final collapse. Levi Bizzee escaped from Andersonville only to suffer capture again much later in the war. He died from disease after exchange. Bartholomew O'Connell also freed himself and returned to his unit only to die in battle just before the fighting ended.

By April 4, 1865, Captain Wirz learned that Federal cavalry had crossed Alabama en route to Georgia. He began organizing transportation and sending his remaining prisoners to the Federal lines at a rate of more than one thousand men per day. On April 7, however, seven men made the last recorded escapes. Gill Sloan likely belonged to that group. Aside from thus missing his chance at almost immediate release, he traveled the whole length of Florida, suffering recapture and escape twice, before staggering into safety at Dry Tortugas. Daniel Bond of the First Minnesota left at the same time. He spent more than a month aided by slaves and Confederate deserters before he reached safety at Apalachicola, Florida. Upon finally reaching safety, Bond wrote, "Joy joy forever, my task is done. The gates are passed, and heaven is now." By the time he reached that point of safety, however, Wirz had sent his remaining prisoners at Andersonville to the Federal lines.

Other prisoners finally escaped when the war ended. They avoided the final problem of escape: that of passing through the Confederate lines. Sergeant John H. White of the 103rd Pennsylvania was one such man. He escaped in April 1865 and found himself wandering over much of Georgia in the last days of the war. Disguised as a Confederate soldier, he even traveled as far north as Dalton, Georgia, near the Tennessee state line. A month after his escape, he finally reached Federal cavalry commanded by General John Wilson.

John Wallace of the Seventh Ohio Cavalry escaped that March and had to travel to Nashville, Tennessee, to reach Federal lines. Thomas H. Howe and other escaped prisoners of war likewise came out of hiding from caves and forests to join the growing population of refugees caught up in the chaos at the end of the war. E.N. Gilpin of the Third Iowa Cavalry, stationed in Macon, wrote about them in his diary on April 23, 1865:

> *Andersonville is so near that the war is a reality indeed with us. Many of our prisoners who have escaped and have been lying out in swamps for months are coming in almost starved and naked. It is horrible the way they were treated.*

Presumably, most of these particular escapees had jumped from trains during transfers from the prison. These men at least had the consolation that, unlike hundreds of the inmates released from Andersonville and other prisons, they avoided dying aboard the civilian troop transport *Sultana* when it exploded on the morning of April 27, 1865. The survivors continued to suffer, however, as a Federal nurse remembered:

> *The hair of some was matted together, like beasts of the stall which lie down in their own filth. Vermin are over them in abundance. Nearly every man was darkened by scurvy, or black with rough scales, and with scorbutic sores. One in particular was reduced to the merest skeleton; his face, neck, and feet were covered with thick, green mold. A number who had government*

clothes given to them on the boat were too feeble to put them on, and were carried ashore partially dressed, hugging their clothing with a death-grasp that they could not be persuaded to yield. It was not infrequent to hear a man feebly call, as he was laid on a stretcher, "Don't take my clothes," "Oh, save my new shoes," "Don't let my socks go back to Andersonville." In their wild death-struggle, with bony arms and hands extended, they would hold up their new socks, that could not be put on because of their swollen limbs, saying "Save 'em till I get home." In a little while, however, the souls of many were released from their worn-out frames, and borne to that higher home where all things are registered for a great day of account.

Escapees from the deadliest prison in American history reached General Sherman and other officers to report on how the men they left behind had lived and died. These men certainly contributed to the respective reports on conditions in Confederate prisons published by a joint congressional committee and by the United States Sanitary Commission. The six hundred Confederate officers used by the Federal military as human shields in the siege of Charleston, South Carolina, had their rations reduced to what fugitives from Andersonville claimed they had received. A number of these men would also serve as witnesses in the postwar trial of Captain Hartmann Heinrich "Henry" Wirz of Andersonville, although only one of them, Jasper Culver, mentioned his escape.

The experiences of Jasper Culver of the First Wisconsin Infantry prove all too typical of his special class of inmates. He tried unsuccessfully to flee captivity in Virginia before receiving a transfer to Andersonville. Once there, Culver, along with Lewis Trowbridge and Thomas D. Mason, escaped and, with the aid of slaves, joined Sherman's army near Atlanta. Despite having kept a diary that he later edited into a memoir in 1923, the few published details of his escape only appear in his regiment's history.

The conditions at Andersonville also proved so bad for the guards that they sometimes joined escaping prisoners. Morgan E. Dowling wrote of a sergeant bribed by prisoners on a work detail to not only allow them to go but also to guide them to the Federal lines. The deserting Confederate even furnished each Yankee with a gun and ammunition. When other guards set out in pursuit, the fleeing men killed most of the dogs. The pursuers withdrew, also with a number of casualties. This may have been the escape on June 10, 1864, wherein John Ransom's friend George Hendryx left in a Confederate uniform, taking with him a gun and a guide from the garrison. It may also have been the escape where Stephen Payne and thirty other inmates bribed a guard. Three nights later, Wirz found seven of the towers empty, the guards having left the stockade with some dozen prisoners, who had gone under the wall via a tunnel. Prisoner John Northrop wrote in his diary about nine men leaving by a tunnel and then escaping with a guard who joined them. William H. Smith wrote in his diary on October 9, 1864, of a man named Hogan, who escaped with four other men, all reportedly armed.

From all of these accounts, the number of men who successfully escaped from Andersonville by the narrowest definition likely comes to only about two dozen. They tended to live long lives afterward, unlike their comrades who survived the prison to return to their homes after the war. DeLayvan R. Streeter, for example, likely the first such escapee, died on March 22, 1932. By contrast, fewer than one in forty of the men who entered Andersonville still lived as late as 1890, according to one of their number. Curiously, none of the men who actually did escape wrote a book, went on a speaking tour or otherwise promoted his great adventure. They may have had what historian Robert Doyle defined as mental "fire walls."

Within all of these stories, some answers emerge on why none of the escapees of Andersonville promoted his adventures. Some of the men who published their memoirs did so, in part, out of the shame of capture and to explain why they failed to escape. Many of these soldiers claimed, probably falsely, to have tried to reach the Federal lines numerous times, only to meet defeat from bad luck and circumstances. Prisoners of war commonly share such guilt, all the more so when they feel they have somehow failed in a victorious cause where other men came home as heroes. Men who succeeded in escaping avoided these problems and thus lacked that motive to write a book. Other soldiers, such as Hoopes, lacked a story long enough to profitably tell. Some former prisoners, such as Farmer, likely preferred to keep the details of their escapes secret while they lived. The men Agnes Spencer and other Southerners saved surely chose to avoid compromising their benefactors by publicizing the names of Southern residents who gave help to fugitive Yankees.

The small number of truly successful escapees, perhaps only two dozen men, also seems to have worked against any of them stopping long enough in their later lives to write a book. Andersonville prisoner Henry M. Davidson all but succeeded in his escape attempt, and he did, after his exchange, publish a thick book that covered his flight in detail. He had an exceptional reason, however, to publish his adventures. Davidson and other former prisoners, such as Robert H. Kellogg, quickly put their works out in order to compel the public to lobby the Federal government to obtain the exchange of all Federal soldiers and sailors held in the South. In this way, he and other survivors sought to bring about the greatest escape of all: the safe release of all of the imprisoned.

Many of these men who got out did so as only one incident in their lives of escape, supporting the theory that they had a form of psychosis, which Israeli satirist and general Shimon Tzabar called barbed wire disease. They would not accept confinement. Witnesses remembered that Native Americans at Andersonville died at an exceptionally high rate, almost certainly from being unable to take the confinement.

Some men avoided returning to the restrictive life of the Federal military, leaving them to risk arrest as deserters. John B. Hotchkiss of Brooklyn, New York, escaped from Andersonville with a plan to reach Cuba as a sailor on blockade runner. Lost in the swamps, however, he became deranged and forgot his past. Hotchkiss claimed that he finally "awoke" in 1888, upon reading a history of his family in New York. He had lived for decades as a prosperous plantation owner named John Schooner in Key West, Florida.

Andersonville escapee Lawrence LeBron, veteran of various adventures as a Federal scout, would survive the war and go on to pursue Indians in the West, chase bandits on the Union Pacific Railroad and deliver mail in Chicago. Private John Bolton of the Seventeenth Indiana Infantry did not stay in Andersonville long. En route to the new Camp Lawton, he escaped while passing through Milledgeville and joined the approaching Federal army. Afterward, while on furlough from his unit, he narrowly missed death when the overcrowded troop car he was riding in turned over. Marrying on August 22, 1868, he would leave his wife and small children to seek work. Without any further communication, he did not return home until 1919. His wife blamed his decades-long absence on his nature of being "forgetful and careless, and of a wandering disposition." Death caught up with him while he was confined at the soldiers' home in Junction City, Kansas, on March 25, 1925.

Numerous efforts were made in the decades after the war to obtain special benefits for the survivors of the Confederate prisons. Dozens of books, prints and lectures were made toward that end, and Andersonville became so prominent in these efforts that many Americans, even to the present day, believe that it was the only Confederate prison, or even the only military prison of the Civil War. Each new work on this prison would build on the facts, rumors and exaggerations of earlier works to create a greater body of Andersonville lore.

Several prisoner of war survivor societies were formed, and pension attorneys, such as George E. Lemon, founder of the veterans' newspaper the *National Tribune* (predecessor of today's *Stars and Stripes*), promoted these efforts to find new business. John McElroy, Andersonville survivor and author of the major memoir of the prison, became editor of the *Tribune* and even one of several professional prisoner of war survivors. He also wrote a novel and a humorous satire about the prison.

Escape accounts, highlighted with tales of the adventure of avoiding capture, became especially popular. Charles Mather Smith's account of his escape, for example, received nationwide attention in the 1890s when he went on tour as a speaker and displayed artifacts from his escape. A Rhode Island officers' organization of veterans later published the story of Smith's escape.

Not having actually escaped or even having been at Andersonville proved no hindrance to publishing a personal escape memoir. Joseph Keen, Hiram S. Daskam and Thomas H. Howe wrote their respective books with "Escape from Andersonville" as part of the titles. These books only dealt with their adventures after jumping from trains that had taken them away from the camp. Morgan E. Dowling took advantage of the Andersonville market to write romantic historical escape fiction around his real experiences as a prisoner. This tale, which he promoted as all fact, has a heroine who follows him to the prison. Englishman James Gillespie's account of his various escape attempts suspiciously resembles the known experiences of other prisoners. Ralph O. Bates went on a national lecture tour about what he claimed was his service as a teenager in the Ninth Ohio Cavalry, his imprisonment in Camp Sumter, a daring escape with a friend, an interview with President Lincoln and his testimony in the trial of Captain Wirz, none of which actually happened. His widow published his purely imaginary memoirs, which a critic described as expounding "bad fiction as fact."

5

THE HANGING OF THE RAIDERS

One of the most famous incidents in the history of Camp Sumter (Andersonville) was the execution of six of the prisoners as murderers and thieves by their fellow inmates. What happened there on the afternoon of July 11, 1864, was very different from the morality tale that some writers would want us to believe. In their primitivism version of the executions story, some prisoners of war from the worst areas of New York City were driven by the horrid conditions in the prison to steal from and even to kill their fellow inmates for survival. When their raiding became intolerable to their fellow prisoners, the victims rioted and turned the raiders over to Captain Henry Wirz, the Confederate officer in charge of the interior of the prison, for confinement. Wirz announced, however, that he would release the captives, leaving the inmates to try and punish their comrades. They held trials, had their decisions approved by General Sherman and conducted the executions of the men who had been condemned.

This legendary, in parts even mythical, version of the real execution of the raiders would come to be held up as an example of the enduring power of rule of law and justice rising above barbarism. The contrast of this desperate, ad hoc–enforcement rule of law represented to some observers the moral superiority of the North's free labor society over the slavery and class-oriented South. The story perpetuated negative stereotypes of New York's Irish population, from which the raiders came, and it countered the image of the Civil War prisoners of war as shirkers, "coffee boilers" or cowards trying to avoid danger in battle, unlike the

Limber Jim hanging the raiders at Andersonville. *Courtesy of the Andersonville National Historic Site.*

heroes of an otherwise victorious military fighting for a righteous cause. They were among the veterans satirized by the Cowardly Lion character in Frank Baum's *Wizard of Oz* children's books. Prisoner of war associations used this version of the story of the hangings at Andersonville in their unsuccessful national campaigns to obtain special government benefits for former prisoners.

This legendary hero epic also contains a mystery: the identity of the executioner, a man known as "Limber Jim." Different prisoners gave varying names and other details about this character. Knowing the true identity of this man amounts to more than historical trivia. The search for him as a real person says much about the history of the United States and the faction of the population that lived on the fringe of society and often beyond contemporary records. Limber Jim's name suggests such a shadow person. An acrobat, freak, long-limbed man or exceptional horse could be called a "limber Jim." Prisoner Melvin Grigsby remembered him as having been with a circus. The word "limmer" meant mongrel and may have placed this man in society's marginal classes. The term "limber" also referred to the holes cut in a ship's deck to drain the pumps and to the limber of a field artillery piece. An enigmatic folk song about a Limber Jim and the Battle of Shiloh emerged from the Civil War.

Such people often appear only in legend and theory but there they may disappear. Limber Jim, for example, allegedly had a brother, perhaps in the Confederacy's Cahawba Prison but otherwise unidentified, who died at the hands of the bandits who would become the raiders at Andersonville. Some of those accounts, and others, have the thieves mugging Jim while he had his pants down. In different stories, he appears as a concerned prisoner, a popular trader and even as leader of a gang of raiders. As the last figure, Limber Jim turned on his fellow bandits to save himself from punishment by an uprising of the victims. In all accounts, including the one in John Frankenheimer's 1996 movie *Andersonville*, he acts as a hero who organizes his fellow inmates to stop the raiders. He persuades Captain Wirz to give his followers clubs with which to strike back at the bandits. Throughout all of these tales, crowds of prisoners, guards and onlookers see him late in the afternoon of July 11, 1864, personally hanging William "Mosby the Raider" Collins, the man who robbed him.

Even if the basic facts of Limber Jim at Andersonville are true, he may have deliberately chosen to elude historians, or at least the friends of the men he helped to hang. The Civil War came about at the beginning of the widespread use of the nom de plume by the American public. Novelist Herman Melville used the term "confidence man" (e.g. con man) in 1849, but its use spread rapidly through the new expanding transportation system of locomotives and steamboats, allowing persons to commit fraud, steal identities or literally reinvent themselves. Proof of identity in those years consisted of little more than personal recommendations that could be forged or bought. Credit reporting agencies, private detectives and city directories would emerge in this period to protect the wary, but essentially, outside of one's community, a person could be anyone he or she claimed to be. An individual could become an entirely new person and could even assume the appearance of someone of the opposite sex. Mental illness and, in those years, little-understood drugs such as laudanum also encouraged personality and even identity changes. Public faith in people who had the appearance of middle-class respectability suffered.

Even persons who remained at home could be different persons to different people depending on circumstances, such as the famous William Brodie of Edinburgh, the basis for the central character in Robert Louis Stevenson's novel *The Strange Case of Dr. Jekyll and Mr. Hyde*. The armies of the Civil War expanded the opportunity of assuming a new life, especially when a soldier could enlist, desert and reenlist under a different name multiple times to collect bounty money. The man who hanged the raider Collins may have been remembered as Limber Jim because he never told his fellow prisoners his real name, or he may not have had any name other than "Limber Jim." Some Limber Jims may have been the inventions of alleged Andersonville survivors seeking to sell books. The legendary character is likely a composite of several real men. He has appeared in scholarly histories, although MacKinlay Kantor did not use him as a character in his Pulitzer Prize–winning novel *Andersonville*, likely because he felt the character was too ambiguous, even for a work of historical fiction. Ironically, at least one of the raider leaders hanged at Andersonville also lived (and died) under a false identity.

As Andersonville historian William Marvel wrote, only when the legends about such tales as the executions and Limber Jim are put aside will the more important history of the prison be allowed to emerge. We can then learn the special lessons that come from the truth, such as why this crude stockade built at an isolated railroad siding resulted in so many men losing their lives. Credible records exist that at least one person called Limber Jim was at Andersonville. For example, William H. Smith wrote in his diary on December 11, 1864, that he visited Limber Jim in the cookhouse, and George W. Fechter mentioned him in his 1865 testimony at the trial of Captain Henry Wirz for war crimes. Even these sources, however, may refer to different men. Only one real person, whatever his name or story, hanged Collins, and any genuine discussion of that real man centers on that event. To find him requires pulling together what credible information exists of the executions to see who, if anyone, matches the accounts of Limber Jim.

Limber Jim had ample reason to want to obscure his real identity, even as he became a legend in the greater saga of America's deadliest prison. He belonged to one or both of Andersonville's two different economies, both of which preyed on the starving, sick and ragged prisoners. Guards and prisoners allowed to leave the stockade would trade with local farmers for groceries. This business brought in enough food to keep prisoners, and even guards, with something to trade from starving. W.B. Hibbs remembered one prisoner businessman beginning with only a button but leaving the prison in March 1865, accompanied by Limber Jim, with $3,000. Critics of these "western" swindlers claimed that desperate men were gouged in this trade as the men who had nothing left to trade starved to death around them. John H. Morris of Herkimer County, New York, the civilian ship owner captured with Captain Herbert Hunt on the coast of North Carolina in what was apparently a smuggling scheme that was illegal in both warring nations, had special success as an Andersonville entrepreneur. He would buy checks and bonds for pennies on the Confederate dollar from desperate inmates in Southern prisons. With at least Confederate cooperation, Morris profitably crossed the lines of the opposing armies to further this scheme.

Limber Jim would be remembered as the king of these merchants and bankers; he was so successful that he ran Andersonville. Different veterans wrote of him as a gigantic Pennsylvanian or as being from Illinois or Kentucky. POW memoirist Melvin Grigsby wrote that he was a "tall, slim, wiry man, good looking, good hearted, full of energy, a lover of fun," whom others described as standing on boxes and barrels to draw crowds with jokes, stories and songs, supposedly while wearing a large sombrero, red shirt and artilleryman's pants. He hired Ezra Ripple to entertain the audience with violin playing for doughnuts and his root or sour beer. The latter became Limber Jim's great product, which he promoted as a treatment for the scurvy that proved fatal to vast numbers of his fellow prisoners. It was made from corn mush fermented with molasses in a barrel given to him by Captain Wirz. Limber Jim made the taste bearable by adding sassafras roots from the prison's swamp. He sold it for five cents per cup, more than the cost for a barrel of his sometimes fly-infested "cure." Limber Jim operated from a stand on Main Street, opposite the north gate, lived in a large board shanty nearby and ran his gambling in a tent that held twelve or more men. His entourage armed itself with clubs and knives, and he hired two physically imposing men as personal bodyguards.

The raiders of Andersonville were remembered by the inmates as thugs from the gangs of New York City and the camp's other economic entity: organized crime. Some of the survivors also remembered the "westerner" Limber Jim as a raider leader, at least when it profited him. Such thieves had organized earlier at the Belle Island and Cahawba Prisons. Their organization and activities transferred in tact to the new Confederate Camp Sumter (Andersonville) in February 1864.

For these men, surviving by thievery and even murder in a place like a Confederate prison would not have been any different than surviving in their civilian lives in a place like New York's notorious Five Points. "Fresh fish," Andersonville slang for men so new that they did not yet stink, would be robbed by individual raiders or small groups of thieves who used darkness, tents or crowds as cover from the guards. One scam involved arranging for an exchange for a blanket or some other item of value. The thieves would then rob the victim while covering their crime by screaming that he tried to rob them. One corpse was reportedly found buried in the raider's camp, and Leroy L. Key told of a camp surgeon who believed that some seventy-five men had died from being bludgeoned by the raiders. These gangs demanded goods and money from the camp's merchants, and they reportedly bragged that they would own everything in the stockade by July 4. Key remembered that the raiders became so bold that they began to rob even the wagons that brought in the inadequate rations for the whole prison, thereby threatening all of the prisoners.

Another view of the raiders, like the alternative negative opinion of Limber Jim, presents a different answer for these men, if not an excuse for their crimes. Patrick Delaney, as he stood ready to be executed for being a raider, would claim that he found the prison bearable only by robbing the new prisoners; otherwise, he would rather die. New York prisoner Robert Knox Sneden, a well-off Andersonville prisoner at least sympathetic to the raiders, wrote of these men as being so impoverished that they lived in holes on "Raider's Island" in the swampy middle ground of the prison. The few other defenders of the raiders described them as driven to stealing to survive. Theft of money and other belongings from a prisoner, however, could condemn that soldier to a slow and hard death by starvation.

The prisoners never just stood by while they and the fresh fish were treated as prey. Peter "Big Pete" Aubrey organized a defensive gang as early as April 1864. Leroy Key formed thirteen self-defense companies of thirty men and one elected captain in each, although such organizations were reportedly infiltrated by the raiders. Critics argued that these men were not police forces as much as they were tribes that sometimes were only marginally different from the raiders. As early as May 22, 1864, James Burton wrote in his Andersonville diary of a captured raider having half of his head shaved and being otherwise humiliated. John L. Hoster remembered such actions as becoming routine. On the night of June 28, when a group of raiders attacked a tent near Hoster, the whole "neighborhood" rose up and beat off the bandits.

This classic competition over the same prey between the swindler merchants/gamblers and the raiders forced the camp's authorities to finally take action in June 1864. Prisoner James Burton wrote that a raider stabbing and mortally wounding a sergeant from an Illinois regiment finally brought the problem of crime inside the stockade to a head. Prisoner John Urban, alias John G. Dowd, and others, however, wrote that Urban started the final chain of events that led to the end of the raiders when he complained to Confederate captain Henry Wirz about his watch being stolen. Wirz had command of the interior of the stockade and the distribution of rations to prisoners, but not much else. He seemed to be the only person in the prison who felt no fear in the stockade and would ride among the prisoners unarmed. Wirz discussed the situation with the prisoners and kept them from rushing the wall. He chided them for allowing perhaps fifty bandits to rob and kill from a prison population of some twenty-six thousand.

Captain Wirz took it upon himself to end the disorder within the stockade. He ordered an end to the distribution of rations until the inmates stopped the robberies. The thieves threatened to make even worse the near riot situation that frequently occurred when the gates were opened for the ration wagon. It took two days of no food at all before a delegation of Aubrey, Key and probably others, including Limber Jim, came forward to Wirz to request clubs and armed soldiers for use in arresting the raiders. They likely had been reluctant to act because Wirz, in imposing rule of law among the prisoners, might be bad for their own questionable business. Also, the definition of "raider" was so hazy that they or their friends might be collected in the roundup of the camp's criminal element.

The fears of the merchant prisoners proved justified. Inmates cheered as Wirz, Key and others led the guards in the arrest of the raiders. Inmates, surprisingly, could identify only a few of the miscreants, but more names were forced from the men who were caught until eighty-four accused bandits were apprehended. Of that number, the guards kept only fourteen of the reportedly worst men. The rest of the raiders were turned over to the other prisoners for a beating as they ran between two rows of the inmates, a punishment that reportedly killed three of the raiders.

Captain Wirz, however, refused to take any responsibility for the punishment of the bandits. He did persuade his superior and the camp's commandant, Brigadier General John H. Winder, to authorize the prisoners to try the raider leaders. Pete McCullough of the Eighth Missouri Infantry served as the judge in the subsequent trial. Prisoner Henry C. "Romeo" Higginson, no friend of the raiders, still served as their defense attorney, at their request. Raider Pete Bradley looked for witnesses for the defense. Sergeant Otis W. Carpenter of the Seventh Michigan Cavalry, Higginson's messmate, served as prosecutor. Few of the defendants were found guilty, and most of the convicted were sentenced only to beatings and related punishment. The six worst offenders were sentenced to death by hanging.

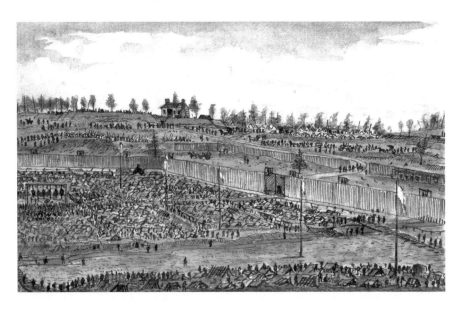

This page: Prisoner Robert Knox Sneden drew from memory the gallows that hanged the infamous raiders of Andersonville and the gathering for their execution on July 11, 1864. *Courtesy of the Virginia Historical Society.*

Higginson, their attorney, arranged for the executions, and McCullough, their judge, smuggled in the wood for the gallows, although Captain Wirz arranged for its construction. No one identified as Limber Jim appears in the surviving court records.

Only in the often-questionable prison memoirs does the character of Limber Jim agree to serve as the executioner. Critics claim that he acted in order to keep from being punished as a raider himself or because of an unfulfilled promise from Wirz that he would be released.

On July 11, 1864, the executions took place while crowds, in legend said to have numbered in the tens of thousands, looked on and the militia served as extra security. The prison's cannons were prepared to sweep the stockade if a riot broke out, although the garrison's artillerymen ignored Wirz's frantic pleas to open fire. (Wirz had no authority over the guards or garrison.) Condemned raider Charles Curtis pulled a knife and fought his way through the crowd of prisoners. Pursuers chased him to a hole, where he tried to hide under a dead prisoner for some two hours. The mob beat him before Joseph Alvis Jordan, Hiram Grow and Joseph C. Maxson of Company C of the Eighty-fifth New York Infantry finally returned him to the gallows. Charles Curtis, Patrick Delaney (an alias, real name not known), Cary Sullivan (aka W. Rickson), Andrew Munn (or Muir), William Collins (alias William Wrixon) and John Sarsfield then stood ready to die.

According to legend, Limber Jim personally hanged William "Mosby" Collins, if not all of the raider leaders. The floor fell from under the six condemned men as the crowd roared. The rope around Collins's neck broke—or, according to one source, Limber Jim cut him loose—and Collins fell to the ground. A man near the gallows reportedly asked if that meant that Collins was innocent, to which Limber Jim supposedly replied, "Not by a d--n sight!" A mob quickly subdued Collins and brought him back to the gallows. Andersonville storytellers would relate how Collins offered his hangman $1,000 for his life. Limber Jim, however, replied, "The rope around your neck cost me $176 [the amount Collins had stolen from him], and I will hang you as long as I can tie a knot in it." He then restored the gallows with enough rope to complete the last execution.

The prisoners had mixed feelings about these events. Martin S. Harris of the Fifth New York Artillery wished that ten times more of the raiders could have been hanged. Henry E. Olinger of the Twentieth Indiana Infantry, however, wrote that "it was no doubt, justice, but it was an impressive Sight to me that I never care to witness again." Key, along with Goody Larkin,

Jim Johnson, Ned Carringan, Limber Jim, George W. Fechter and Abel Wadsworth "Wad" Payne subsequently formed a prisoner police force that the prisoners called the "regulators." They forced sergeants to take care of the sick, keep the camp clean, improve the marsh area, clear the streets and end thievery. Critics, however, claimed that the new constabulary extracted double rations and taxes as payment for their civil services while including former raiders in their ranks. One prisoner remembered that their leader (Limber Jim?) accompanied the prison's dog packs in tracking down escapees and reported on escape tunnels. Another survivor remembered Limber Jim having men whipped in front of his tent and passing in and out of the stockade with abandon. In October 1864, the prisoners rose up and rioted against the regulators.

The executions of the raiders at Andersonville did happen, and their basic facts can be found in the stories, but so little with credibility comes from the tales of Limber Jim that hardly any proof of a real man exists. Finding his identity has been compounded by so many different claims that sound compelling but come from writers who falsely made themselves out to appear more important by claiming to have known all of the important characters in the tragedy of Andersonville. Other men confused and misidentified Limber Jim with other men in the prison's history, such as Leroy L. Key. Almost everyone who played a major role in the trial of the raiders was identified in later years as Limber Jim. Information pieced together from different sources solidly identify him as James McLaughlin (or McGlaughlin) of the Sixty-seventh Illinois Infantry (ninety-day men) and later a sergeant in the First Illinois Light Artillery. McLaughlin, however, only became a Confederate captive on November 27, 1864, long after the raider executions. The real Limber Jim likely took that identity—and the identities of other men, too—to hide his past or to get extra rations.

Michael Regan of the Sixty-ninth New York spent no time at Andersonville but claimed to have known Limber Jim as a "tunnel traitor" (informant to the guards) at Cahawba Prison who would die in a gunfight in Cheyenne, Wyoming, on September 16, 1867. The man Regan described may have been Thomas J. Goodman, a civilian with a previous military record supported by men who knew Limber Jim and who did participate in the executions of the raiders. Goodman did not die in Cheyenne in 1867 but, in his pension claim, stated that he escaped from Andersonville while known as Limber Jim, only to be recaptured and later exchanged.

Henry Harrison Rood published a history of his Company A of the Thirteenth Iowa Infantry Regiment in 1889 and, eight years later, gave a paper in which he identified his hustler and scrounger subordinate Vincent Ferguson Stevens as the famous Limber Jim of Andersonville. Stevens himself told of his experiences as the notorious camp hangman at a talk before the Nebraska convention of the Grand Army of the Republic in 1897. By then, however, few survivors of Andersonville remained who might have challenged his claims.

With so many possibilities and no undeniable proof, the identity of Limber Jim may appear to be just an example of the problems of false identity in mid-nineteenth century America. He and his notoriety, however, tell us more. Writers for the respective partisan press of the Civil War, the prosecution of Henry Wirz, the memoir writers after the war and other images of Andersonville became stronger than the truth. Limber Jim became a myth that was part of the greater legend of Andersonville. Such accounts became falsehoods that too often have replaced fact. The real man was a product of the new era of new or stolen identities, exacerbated by the Civil War, wherein even notable men sometimes had to hide their pasts and live within legends and incredulous truth.

6

TWILIGHT AT ANDERSONVILLE

Most of the horrors at Andersonville came to an end not because of the negative reports by the Confederate inspectors, the public complaints or simple humanity. They ended because of the fall of Atlanta and the potential for General Sherman's army arriving at the gates of the prison. Ironically, despite pleas from the families of the inmates of America's most notorious stockade, Major General William T. Sherman did little to nothing to help the prisoners. He claimed that the best thing he could do for them would be to end the war as soon as possible, beginning with the race across Georgia that became his famous March to the Sea. He bypassed the virtually undefended Andersonville by hundreds of miles.

William Tecumseh Sherman did have reasons to have acted differently. For years, newspapers carried stories and illustrations of the horrors of such infamous prisons as Andersonville. Some 11 percent of the total Federal military's wartime mortality came from the captives of the Confederates. Escaped prisoners even met with Sherman to plead for the release of the prisoners by any means. William Whipple, a railroad conductor who passed the prison frequently, reported on the horrors there to Federal officers. Sherman received one hundred letters a day from families of prisoners asking him to save their kinsmen. The political value of such a rescue for the Lincoln administration would be incalculable for the national elections that November.

The general chose not to use Andersonville to become a hero, but he had no qualms about using the prison as a weapon as he prepared to hurl his armies against Georgia in the spring of 1864. By the following August, the camp's underfed population of prisoners had swelled to 33,006. The Confederacy had only some 900 to 2,500 old men, boys and inexperienced regulars to guard Andersonville. Many of the garrison wanted to escape as much as the men they watched.

If those Yankees were freed, however, the largest group of desperate men in the world would be released upon a largely defenseless civilian population of Georgia. Sherman's modernist theories of fear as a weapon that imposes generational scars would have been realized on a grand scale. Soldiers would have deserted from what remained of the Southern armies to return home to protect their families. Thousands of slaves would have aided in and joined in the great escape. Georgia's railroads and the arsenals of Augusta, Columbus and Macon were almost all that remained of the South's industrial resources outside of Richmond by 1864. The resulting damage from the Andersonville rampage would have been far greater than the rather limited damage to personal property that Sherman's army actually accomplished.

The truth of Sherman and Andersonville, like seemingly everything else in the general's life, lies buried beneath complexities that belong in the realms of psychohistory. Like Andersonville, this "general who marched to hell" and the "merchant of terror" has been demonized in Civil War lore beyond historical realities. His failure to rescue the prisoners held by the Confederacy became one of the lesser crimes in the Sherman legends. He has been falsely credited with burning Atlanta, destroying a swath of Georgia sixty miles wide and with the deliberate destruction of Columbia, South Carolina. Scholarship does not sustain those charges but proves them to be, at best, grossly exaggerated. The general did deliberately wage a war of terrorism, but as a war of popular fear with little of the damage to property and the civil disorder that he found so personally repugnant. He wanted to create a societal opposition that would define what he called "rebellion" for generations to come. The real Sherman regarded as repugnant harming civilians, civil disobedience, land mines and exploding bullets. When he learned of his own prisoners being reduced to starvation rations in retaliation for what was fed to Andersonville's inmates, Sherman ordered full rations restored to them.

Prisoners at Andersonville believed that Sherman's cavalry would soon be coming to their rescue. Instead of being killed by the garrison, the inmates envisioned their guards fleeing and the local people becoming hostages. Rousseau's successful cavalry raid in Alabama in July 1864 was mistakenly believed to have been such an attempt at rescue. On July 27, 1864, as Sherman besieged Atlanta, he did send his blue-clad five thousand cavalrymen on a raid against the city's rail lines with the lesser objective of also rescuing the Federal officers held in Camp Oglethorpe in Macon and the enlisted men in Camp Sumter (Andersonville) at Anderson Station. After a series of battles with militia, state troops and General Joseph Wheeler's Rebel cavalry, the great raid failed, with almost one thousand troopers ending up as prisoners, not liberators. Sherman would take responsibility for this defeat and would call approving the attempt to rescue the prisoners of war a mistake. Georgians, however, became frightened at the prospect of the release of thirty thousand Federal prisoners. The general would later send his cavalry to try to find the prison camp at Blackshear, Georgia, but by that time, those men were back at Andersonville. Late in the war, after Andersonville had been largely evacuated and reduced to a prisoner hospital, mysterious cavalrymen were still reported in the neighborhood.

The men captured in the great raid would be exchanged, but the inmates they left behind in Andersonville had no reason for gratitude. In one account, General Sherman turned down a chance to trade his prisoners for the sick Union soldiers brought near his lines for exchange. Upon learning that they would be returned to Andersonville, supposedly 150 of these Federals still managed to escape. In truth, some soldiers who were not among Sherman's horsemen had slipped into the previously mentioned exchange of cavalrymen, and at least some of them did reach the Federal lines. The general did unsuccessfully try to trade 1,000 Atlanta civilians whom he had confined for their part in the Southern war effort for an equal number of soldiers held by the Confederates.

A myth started that emaciated escapees from Andersonville reached Sherman's army in Milledgeville while the last of his soldiers were sitting down to enjoy a Thanksgiving dinner. These ragged skeletons of men pleaded for immediate rescue of the thousands of their sick friends still at Camp Sumter. The general and his army, however, continued on to Savannah, leaving the inmates at Andersonville to their fate. (Sherman did leave twenty-six of his sick men behind at Milledgeville.) Those blue legions and their commander marched to glory and into history without being encumbered with sick and wounded men, escaped prisoners or freed slaves. Other soldiers told similar tales.

What pathetically little Sherman did do for the prisoners at Andersonville would have so hurt his reputation that the first editors of his papers omitted any references to the prison. The omissions include his news to the prisoners that they would soon be released, even as he intended to leave them behind to suffer months more imprisonment or death. He did contact private sources to send those starving men a supply of combs, barber shears and underwear so that they could feel better about being soldiers. Later, the men Sherman left behind at Anderson Station would produce books, interviews, lecture tours, panoramic prints and POW associations. They would promote the horrors of the prison, the alleged crimes of Henry Wirz and their sacrifices, but they would fail to thank Sherman for his contribution to their story.

Sherman could show concern for the plight of others, but only within the narrow confines of the self-imposed rules he used to govern his world. He did take action, within limits that sometimes only he understood, concerning the prisoners of war, civilian refugees, unionist guerrillas and escaped slaves; these actions would often go beyond crushing their hopes to placing them in mortal danger. Emancipation, total war, national politics or revenge did not exist in his universe. Appreciating his reputation, he would write of the thousands of people he presumed wished him in hell.

The camp's guards did not, by themselves, prevent the greatest prison escape of the Civil War as the prisoners let themselves out to join Sherman. More important to keeping the prisoners inside the crude palisade would be the distance to safety, the prospect of rescue or exchange if they waited and the threat of the camp's garrison sweeping the interior of the stockade with cannon fire. The garrison, strengthened with local militiamen, made demonstrations of force in May and July in answer to reports of plans by the emancipated prisoners to rush the walls. Slaves were put to work to keep that palisade from simply being pushed down. The artillerymen fired a cannon into the unoccupied swamp in prison as a warning of what would happen if the walls were rushed. New areas were marked with white flags as a warning against gatherings that would not be tolerated.

The Confederacy, however, would not just let the prisoners go while any chance remained of exchanging them for its own men held in the North, no matter what it cost the South of its dwindling resources. When Confederate general Joseph E. Johnston urged the transfer of the inmates farther to the rear, the Confederate government saw this request as a plan to abandon Atlanta—Sherman's primary objective and the "Gate City" to the Confederate interior and Andersonville. Johnston would be replaced shortly afterward. Ironically, he would claim that he had been forced to defend the city chiefly to stop the release of the prisoners at Andersonville.

Over eleven thousand of the inmates went to Camp Lawton at Millen, Georgia, a new forty-two-acre prison that had almost all of the amenities that Andersonville fatally lacked. The new camp had a free-flowing, clean water stream divided into sections for drinking, bathing and sanitation; a supply depot for gathering and stockpiling provisions; and an interior with ample space, trees and even brick baking ovens for the prisoners. One survivor remembered that he and his fellow inmates received twice the daily rations issued at Andersonville.

Captain Daniel Washington Vowles, an officer at Andersonville, became the commandant at Camp Lawton, and he contributed to the improved conditions there. This Virginia-born veteran of six battles in four states had been brought to Georgia to investigate reports that the Federal prisoners at Andersonville Prison included spies sent by Sherman to work in conjunction with local people in overthrowing the guards at the prison camp.

The captain used his experiences to make Lawton the model for the best and most humane in Confederate prisons, despite what he and his brother Newton had suffered in the harsh conditions of the war in Missouri. Inmates remembered him as a humane man, a good disciplinarian and a competent administrator. When a riot nearly broke out during an attempt to enlist prisoners into the Confederate army, Vowles diffused the situation by ordering the guards out of the stockade and closing the gates. After the war, Vowles would have the distinction of being the one major prison official who survived but escaped arrest. He died in Fowler, Illinois, near where he had recruited men for the Confederate army early in the war and where he had been a doctor, on August 14, 1919. His obituary in the *New York Times* mentioned his time as a prewar mercenary in Nicaragua, serving as a Confederate officer in Missouri and as a messenger in the U.S. Senate but nothing of his time at Andersonville or Millen.

As the new prison proved to be in the path of Sherman's advancing armies, the inmates were again moved beyond rescue to other prisons at Blackshear, Georgia; Florence, South Carolina; and Salisbury, North Carolina, places among the worst Civil War prisons in their horrors. The balance of the remaining Andersonville survivors on the move went to Savannah for parole and release.

Moving these sick and starved Yankees became more important than using this same transportation to feed the South's starving soldiers and civilians, reflecting the strange priorities of a failing bureaucracy. Similar to other such collapsing organizational systems throughout history, the Confederate government now survived only in order to continue to exist beyond any practical benefit to its people or credible hope of success. Some prisoners survived Belle Island, near Richmond, and even Andersonville, to travel on to such places as Salisbury and Vicksburg. They thus moved over more of the Confederate nation than any member of either army. Georgia writer Rebecca Latimer Felton would remember a train load of these men being moved:

> *On that trip we passed car-loads of Andersonville prisoners being removed to another camp as it was expected that Sherman would strike for Andersonville. The night was gloomy and the torch fires made a weird scene as our train rolled along beside passing flat cars on which those Federal prisoners were guarded, with torch lights illuminating the faces of those ragged, smoke begrimed, haggard and miserably filthy men. I had a glimpse of war conditions that was new to me. Prison treatment of such men has always been a disgrace to Christianity and civilization. I had read of Camp Chase and Johnson's Island and been angered at the treatment accorded to our Confederate prisoners, but the sight of train-loads of Federal prisoners on that wild night in Southern Georgia, when I could look into their faces within a few feet of the train I became an eye witness to their enforced degradation, filth and utter destitution and the sight never could be forgotten.*

This terrible journey of the suffering prisoners of war only ended with the conclusion of the war. Ironically, Camp Sumter (Andersonville) opened in late February 1864 because of the danger of Federal cavalry releasing the prisoners in Richmond's Belle Island. Both the Confederate capital and Anderson Station, however, would remain prisons that were never breached long after the other stockades had fallen, essentially to the end of the war.

Most of the men who remained at Andersonville were inmates who were too sick to survive transfer. Only 8,218 soldiers were still at Andersonville at the end of September, and half of those men remained in the prison at the end of October. They numbered so few that the prison finally had a supportable population. Eventually, a hospital, a bakery, some barracks and other amenities went up, proving that the prison was never intended as a facility for exterminating prisoners of war out of sight of Federal protests. The camp administration even abolished the dead line. General Howell Cobb tried to confiscate the prison's newly acquired lumber for the

Confederate hospitals in Macon, but Wirz managed to keep the boards for prisoner housing. Cobb, however, praised the Andersonville captain for his efficiency, as did other inspecting officers. After the Federal army moved on from Georgia, the Confederate government also returned thousands of its prisoners to Andersonville from the open-ground prison at Blackshear, Georgia. They returned to Andersonville in worse shape than when they left. Consequently, Andersonville kept a high mortality rate to the end of the war.

Brigadier General John H. Winder, as commander of the Confederate prisons east of the Mississippi River and Andersonville's commandant, made a number of efforts to end the tragedy at the prison for all of the persons involved. In August 1864, for example, he allowed prisoners Henry C. Higginson, Edward Bates, Sylvester Noirto, Abraham Barns, W.H. Bynon, Jacob Harbauer and Prescott Tracy to return to the North with a petition signed by the camp's sergeants that pleaded for the resumption of the exchange of prisoners as a means of saving the inmates of Andersonville. They met with President Lincoln, and the long and tortuous process began that eventually resulted in an exchange of the prisoners.

As 1864 became 1865, the two warring governments moved toward a general exchange of prisoners, although this effort came too late for most of the captives of Andersonville. On December 31, 1864, Winder urged his Confederate superiors to release any Federals who agreed to abstain from military service until exchanged and also those men whose enlistments had run out. General Grant warned against releasing healthy Confederates to fight again, as he pointed out that it would be inhumane to the soldiers they could kill. At the same time, in February 1865, he also authorized the exchange of prisoners as quickly as possible. By March 1865, Andersonville's administration could begin returning its almost five thousand remaining prisoners to the Federal lines.

The same kinds of bureaucratic incompetence, social indifference and transportation problems that had made the prison such a place of misery now worked to force these men into one last nightmare that would include further confinement and more Andersonville-related deaths. An agreement to dispatch the western soldiers to Camp Fisk, four miles from Vicksburg, and the easterners to Baldwin, near Jacksonville, Florida, broke down, as the garrison auctioned places on the first trains—those cars that took men to the West. The "fortunates" who won this chance of first release took a complex odyssey along the Civil War South's different-gauge, worn-out railroads.

After traveling by train, foot and water, they finally arrived near Vicksburg. By then, they had gone without a meal for three days. Even then, they had to wait at Camp Fisk, with thousands of their comrades, until at last the opposing sides could arrange for their final release. In one of the final ironies of a long list of bizarre circumstances, the last prison camp for holding Union soldiers, sailors and civilians was officially operated by the Confederacy but supplied by the Union, just outside of the Federally occupied Confederate city of Vicksburg, whose Confederate garrison had been allowed to go home upon surrendering in 1863. At least 386 of these Andersonville survivors subsequently died in the explosion of the overcrowded troop transport *Sultana* on April 27, 1865.

Jesse Altom, W.T. Ziegler and 50 of their fellow prisoners signed a parole on April 18, 1865, and took a train to Albany, Georgia. From there, they began a long odyssey by train and on foot that brought them back within sight of the prison, before, abandoned by their guards, they finally reached Federal lines, near Jacksonville, Florida, on April 28. This trek cost at least one prisoner his life and constituted a harrowing escape, although technically these men fail to count officially as either prisoners or fugitives. Michael Heiman and several other men similarly escaped from the prison late in the war. Local people rounded them up and sent them back to Andersonville. With the stockade all but abandoned, they took a train to the Federal forces in Macon. Strictly speaking, they left the prison unopposed. Back at Andersonville, on April 6, Wirz sent 3,424 of his remaining inmates to Albany, Georgia, for later release in Florida. They took what they could carry of their personal belongings and burned the rest. At Albany, the mayor used sentries to keep the guards and the prisoners out of the town. He did present each guard with a Confederate uniform, however.

Unfortunately, they all soon found themselves back where they had started. Lacking any orders about a prisoner release, Federal general Quincy A. Gilmore declined to accept the long-suffering prisoners. Wirz had no authority to let the men go, and doing so might have negatively affected the release of Confederates. (Had Wirz taken that personal initiative, however, he might have later avoided the gallows.) The prisoners next went to Macon, where Wirz planned to transfer them to the Central Railroad for transport to the Federal garrison at Savannah. The arrival of Wilson's Union cavalry caused Colonel George C. Gibbs, Andersonville's new commandant, to order the prisoners back to Anderson Station, even as reports arrived of sightings of Federal cavalrymen only one mile away. In the rush, Captain

Wirz found himself left behind. Finally, Gibbs and Wirz personally escorted their charges to Albany. They then led them and the guards on a three-day march to the railhead at Thomasville, Georgia. From there, they took a train and then made a march to Baldwin, Florida, where Wirz finally released his prisoners.

The sufferings of these men did not end, however. These survivors of Andersonville had to walk still another twenty miles through jungle and swamp to reach the Federal garrison. Some of these ragged, starved men did not survive this last leg of the journey. On May 4, 1865, the last prisoners died at Camp Sumter. The next day, only five sick men and seventeen other Yankees remained in the otherwise abandoned stockade. By then, the guards and local families had looted what military stores remained in the camp. In the interim, other prisoners went to special Federal camps for rehabilitation.

In the popular mind, the Civil War ended with Robert E. Lee's surrender on April 9 or April 26, 1865, in North Carolina, when General Joseph E. Johnston surrendered the remnants of several forces, including the Army of Tennessee, to General Sherman. The Confederate nation, however, would actually hang on a while longer before passing into the twilight of memory, history and legend. The Confederate flag still flew over the ruins of Atlanta until it came down everywhere else. A Confederate convention met in Macon to rebuild tracks torn up by Sherman's troops. Slaves were still being sold in Georgia and, joined by shanghaied freedmen, shipped to Spanish Cuba for resale.

A Rebel flag would also still have waved over Andersonville had the garrison ever been issued one. The camp's mortality rate remained high. The last prisoners were evacuated to Federal lines under the direction of Captain Henry Wirz, the officer in charge of the prisoners. Before the year ended, however, the United States government tried and hanged Wirz as one of the few men, all Confederate, sentenced for war crimes using the notoriously unfair American military tribunal/commission. William Tecumseh Sherman, however, despite what he failed to do for the prisoners he left behind, received a full military review in Washington.

7

AFTER THE GATES CLOSED

Fame is fickle. A small isolated community in southwest Georgia wanted to forget its connection to one of humanity's great disasters but could not escape history, or at least public notoriety. On the other hand, a lawyer who risked his career to defend the "demon of Andersonville" and should be remembered on a level with John Quincy Adams and Clarence Darrow has been worse than forgotten. Despite fighting in one of the most important trials in America's history, he was so miniscule that even his actual name was lost until recent times.

That lawyer defended Hartmann Heinrich "Henry" Wirz, a captain and midlevel functionary in an internment camp where thirteen thousand of some forty thousand individual inmates died of starvation, disease and exposure. Prisoners and historians mistakenly identified Wirz as the commandant of Andersonville Prison, attributing to him powers and authority beyond those of his clerical position. He performed efficiently responsibilities that he should not have had, but he would pay dearly for being the right man in the wrong place. His duties principally consisted of keeping the prison rolls and allowing prisoners to leave the stockade on work details. Arrangements within the walls, such as wells and sanitation, officially fell in the realm of Henry Wirz's responsibilities, and he could decide when, and if, the prisoners received whatever rations had arrived. Guards, while on duty on the stockade wall, could take orders from him. The quantity and quality of the rations, medicine, guards and desperately needed camp improvements were beyond his authority, as attested to by witnesses at his trial. Most of

The press corps that covered the trial of Captain Henry Wirz of Andersonville for a national audience. *Courtesy of the Library of Congress.*

the inmates, however, only had contact with the "Old Dutchman," as the prisoners called the Swiss-born Wirz.

The captain's notoriety, however, threatened his liberty and his life. William Marvel and other researchers have exposed that Wirz created an identity for himself built on questionable claims about his professional training, the circumstances of his arrival in America, his family life and the alleged permanent injuries to his arm. The prosecutor at his trial, by contrast, portrayed him falsely as being an all-powerful commandant of a death camp where he used his nonexistent authority to exercise some mythical control over the garrison, provisions, dogs and medical care to murder helpless prisoners wholesale.

This fictional "demon of Andersonville" murdered individual prisoners, while the real Wirz could not lift his broken and useless pistol. Furthermore, he at least believed that he was in great pain and lay near death. Andersonville Prison existed for little more than fourteen months. Wirz arrived one month after it opened, and he spent much of the rest of the year that followed away from the camp trying to get medical care for his arm. Prisoners frequently heard rumors that he had died.

Quite likely, General Winder gave Wirz, his longtime subordinate, a noncritical position out of pity for the crippled officer. From September 1864 to May 1865, the camp existed as a hospital with a manageable number of prisoners, and Wirz supervised the needed improvements that he and others had tried to make from the beginning. The real Wirz wrote in nearly perfect English, while the war criminal

Henry Wirz. *Courtesy of the Wirz Family Archives, Zurich, Switzerland.*

of legend cursed Yankees in heavily accented, poorly composed English. His notoriety became part of a greater battle of myths wherein the prison's defenders and detractors created mythical Andersonvilles.

Wirz should not have been held to blame for what happened in the real prison. Andersonville's chief administrative officer, commandant Brigadier General John H. Winder, spent much of his time away from the camp. Critics claimed that he never bothered to even see the interior of the stockade, but in truth he suffered "gangrene of the face" from exposure to the prison and his physician ordered him to never return to the Andersonville stockade. Winder, like Wirz, frequently complained about the conditions at the prison to the Confederate government.

Because of the confused and usually absentee administration of the camp, however, Wirz did sometimes find himself the highest-ranking officer present on the prison grounds, even when he had practically no authority. Confederate inspectors described him as an exceptionally competent man, in stark contrast to the bureaucratic bungling and pettiness of other officers at Andersonville. Some prisoners also held him in high regard. His daughter would remember prisoners giving him gifts, some of them handmade. Other survivors described him as a monster that yelled obscenities while inflicting vicious dogs, trigger-happy guards and brutal punishments upon hapless men. Former inmate Prescott Tracy made a deposition, on August 19, 1864, wherein he called Wirz a "brutal monster" who ordered men all but randomly shot. He claimed that the Swiss-born Wirz did give humane treatment to prisoners who, like him, were Germans.

Henry Wirz would write to his superiors about prisoners exaggerating the prison's poor conditions, but the deaths of one-third of the men who entered his stockade spoke far louder to the Northern public than his protests and excuses. The prison that he had the misfortune of being associated with became so infamous that even the prison slang developed by its inmates would eventually become standard Americanisms. That bureaucratic incompetence, economics, geography and technology could produce such an unimaginable "Hell on Earth" as Andersonville, without a conspiracy to murder helpless Union prisoners, was beyond the understanding of Americans then and since.

On May 7, 1865, as only a few former prisoners and some Union medical staff remained around the former Confederate prison camp known popularly as Andersonville, Federal soldiers arrested Henry Wirz. The captain believed that the general amnesty given to Confederate officers included him. He was preparing to travel north in search of work. The arrest took place in front of his wife and children.

Transported to the old Capital Prison in Washington, his trial before a military tribunal began on August 21, 1865. Initially, Captain Wirz had the services of the prestigious Washington law firms of James William Denver, James Hughes and Charles F. Peck, but they backed out when they realized that Wirz would not be receiving a standard criminal trial or court-martial. Hughes felt that the best chance that Wirz had would be to remove any pretence that he would be getting a fair trial. German-born Louis Schade remained to defend the captain, but, while a longtime champion of lost causes, he had almost no training or skill as a courtroom advocate. He had no way to even protest when Secretary of War Edwin Stanton personally read the charges prepared by Judge Advocate Norton Parker Chipman before the court, wherein Wirz was accused of deliberately operating Andersonville as a death camp. Numerous top Confederate leaders, both civilian and military, were also named, but they were never tried for any crimes.

On August 24, Orrin Smith Baker came forward to offer to aid Schade, only to find himself unpaid and essentially the lone attorney for the defense. Born in Orleans, Massachusetts, in 1827, he became a New York lawyer in 1854, although his fortunes during the war had been so reduced that he was a military bounty attorney in Washington when he discovered that the Court of Claims rooms in the Capitol Building had been taken over for the Wirz trial. That he stood for and fought so heroically for this helpless Confederate officer can only be explained by Baker's personal commitment to his profession. He and his wife were outspoken supporters of Abraham Lincoln and the United States' war effort. His brother-in-law had died fighting for the Union cause as an officer, and Baker himself had briefly served in that same military as a lieutenant. Nothing appeared about his past in the extensive coverage of the trial or in anything about this prominent court case in all of the publications that have appeared in the decades since. Playwright Saul Levitt found so little about this attorney that he invented a Maryland lawyer named Otis H. Baker for the historical play *Andersonville Trial*. Scholars of the Wirz trial since have repeated this fiction as fact. The real attorney's death went unnoted in a public hospital for the insane in Napa, California, in 1889.

Orrin Smith Baker (née Obadiah Baker), a Massachusetts-born New York bounty lawyer who despised the Confederacy, gave his all to defend Confederate captain Henry Wirz because Baker believed that everyone deserved a fair trial and an adequate lawyer. He continues to defend Wirz today as the fictional Marylander Otis H. Baker in the award-winning play *Andersonville Trial*. *Author's collection.*

Despite his best efforts and the risk of being held in contempt, Baker argued before a court where the judges had unrestricted privileges to rule on witnesses, arguments, procedure and all others in the trial. Military tribunals and commission trials are not objective judicial proceedings but a means of suppressing or opposing the defense in order to give an appearance of justice to what amounts to a predetermined verdict. Winder died before the war ended and thus was beyond any prosecution by or revenge of the Northern public. Federal prosecutors chose not to prosecute the native-born American officers, politicians and civilians who actually had held the official authority for the food, guards, tracking dogs, materials for shelter, medicine, transportation and other major aspects of the prison. Some of those Americans even appeared as witnesses at Wirz's trial.

The court moved away from any consideration of the civil rights of the defendant but, instead, towards a review of the tragedy of Andersonville. The judge advocate general stacked the commission with men who would find no pity for Wirz. All but one of the nine members of the ruling commission had served on the war's battlefields and one had lost a son in the fighting. Each of these officers also awaited a promotion. In addition, the majority of the board had political ambitions in states with widespread hatred of the Confederacy. The president of the court, General Lewis "Lew" Wallace had served on the military commission that tried and convicted the Lincoln assassins. He had voted them guilty, thus proving that he accepted the validity of military commissions. Wallace privately expressed his conviction of Wirz's guilt, as well as that he wanted the trial over so that he could join a financially lucrative private military campaign in Mexico. Other members of the commission also seemed distracted and, as the trial stretched out over two months, increasingly acted as if wanting to finish this ordeal as quickly as possible for themselves. The effects of the brutal summer heat in the courtroom hardly improved the patience of anyone.

Wartime passions proved enough to bring Wirz to trial, but the German accent of this Roman Catholic also inflamed an Anglo-Saxon Protestant general population with a prejudice against immigrants, Roman Catholics and Germans that preceded the Civil War. Many Americans believed bizarre rumors that the pope had ordered Abraham Lincoln assassinated and that Federal defeats in battle came from cowardly German soldiers. Some bigots associated Wirz with myths of the Swiss Guards as brutal mercenaries. His trial failed to produce any credible account of his acting with personal cruelty or evidence of his role in any conspiracy. Even some prisoners, despite their prejudice against Wirz, would later write of incidences of his kindness to them. Several Andersonville survivors even dared to come forward to defend him at his trial and in print.

The testimony of the prosecution's witnesses only rarely related to Wirz and, at times, came from obvious perjurers. They were allowed to repeat heresy. Some of these men even lied about being at Andersonville. Defense witnesses were interviewed by the prosecutors before testifying, and many of the men who came to defend Wirz were never allowed to take the stand. One potential witness, the prison's baker, James W. Duncan, found himself arrested and later tried for war crimes. (After being sentenced to fifteen years, Duncan would escape from Federal custody in 1867; years later he lived in Pittsburgh, Pennsylvania, and served as a witness in Federal military service pension applications.) The military commission allowed Wirz only 32 of the 106 witnesses Baker requested. Thirty-six other men stood ready to testify for the defense when the court arbitrarily ended the trial after sixty-three brutally hot days.

The best example of the unfairness of Wirz's trial would be the testimony of Ambrose Spencer. A New York–born resident of the Andersonville

Orrin Smith Baker (standing center) defends Captain Wirz (lying on the couch) in the Civil War's only trial of an officer for war crimes. *Author's collection,* Harper's Weekly.

area, Spencer testified at length at Wirz's trial, and he continues to do so today as one of the characters in Levitt's award-winning play *Andersonville Trial*. However, he may have never seen the prison at all or, if he did, only as a temporary guard when the militia had to be called up. Orrin Smith Baker, Wirz's attorney, successfully proved that "Colonel" Spencer, far from being an authority on events at Andersonville and the local agriculture, had actually spent the war away from the prison working for the Confederate government. Wirz himself would denounce Spencer's testimony of hearing incriminating conversations as an outright falsehood. Aside from Ambrose contradicting himself in almost every line of his own testimony, the court should have disqualified him for being a former Confederate official without a pardon and because he was a paid employee of the prosecution. His shady past, if known, would have further damaged his credibility. Spencer would publish a bestselling book based on the testimony, including his own falsehoods, at the Wirz trial. His long life of controversy ended spectacularly

The execution of Captain Henry Wirz on November 10, 1865. Today's Supreme Court building stands on the site of the Wirz execution (the Capital Prison) and across the street from the United States Capitol Building. *Courtesy of the National Archives and Records Administration.*

with his murder in Lynn, Missouri, on April 12, 1876, in a love triangle involving multiple cases of bigamy.

The military tribunal found Captain Wirz guilty, and he strangled to death during his hanging at the future site of the United States Supreme Court building on November 10, 1865, as onlookers yelled for him to remember Andersonville. Wirz wrote a public letter earlier that day to Baker to thank him for all that he had done.

Without Wirz and the prisoners, life went on at the real place of the controversy. Andersonville became not only the popular name of the prison that was officially Camp Sumter, in today's Macon County, Georgia, but also the name of the town that grew up outside of the prison during the Civil War. The now abandoned whistle-stop continues, to the present-day, to serve the people who come, now voluntarily, to visit America's most notorious prison more than a century after the prisoners and guards left. The town grew up with the notoriety of the adjoining Confederate prison. The latter has evolved not only into a symbol of the remembrance of the Civil War but also into a memorial to the sufferings of all American prisoners of war.

The postwar history of that remembrance began on a positive note on October 29, 1866, when Northern missionaries opened a freedman's school for blacks and whites in Camp Sumter's buildings, inadvertently giving back to the local African Americans something in return for the aide they had so often given to escaped prisoners. The Ku Klux Klan, led by Benjamin B. Dykes, however, drove the freedmen from the buildings and from houses they had built for themselves in 1868–69. Dykes had first persuaded the Confederacy

Sections of the walls of the stockade stood for many years and, along with artifacts from the site, were taken as souvenirs. This postwar engraving was made from photographs taken by Engle & Furlong for the Quartermaster Department of the United States Army in 1868. *Author's collection*, Century Magazine.

to build the prison in such an isolated and otherwise inappropriate place. He therefore did the most to create the horrors that followed. He reportedly sold the prison cemetery, if he ever owned it, to a Northern entrepreneur who sought to make a profit from it. After the war, Dykes sued the United States government for wood taken by Federal soldiers from the cemetery property after the war. Federal investigators, in rejecting his claim, wrote that

> *the Army at the capture of the prison, were not in a mood to ask anyone permission to occupy grounds made sacred by the sacrifice in cold blood of over 13,000 Union men...Their humor would have been better suited by hanging claimant, who they might well have believed to have been an aide and abettor in those inhuman wrongs.*

In 1875, the United States government finally purchased the cemetery property from Benjamin Dykes. Despite the opposition from Dykes and other local whites, the freedman's school would continue well into the twentieth century.

Former Confederate colonel Joel R. Griffin, a resident of nearby Fort Valley, started the second phase of the prison's history, under orders from Federal general James Wilson. Griffin prevented Dykes from taking the stockade walls and stopped a plan to grow grapes over the remains of the soldiers. Weather and animals had exposed shallow graves. The colonel had them reburied and started a fence for its cemetery. Prisoner Dorence Atwater had smuggled out a grave register of his fallen comrades. He used this record to help the famous Clara Barton in organizing an expedition to mark the graves in the camp cemetery in July and August 1865. On July 25, 1865, Major James M. Moore, with two companies of United States troops, arrived at Anderson Station to take charge of the cemetery. Hospital buildings were taken over for use by sick ex-Confederates employed by Moore to supervise the laborers who cleaned up the grounds and covered exposed bodies. Some bodies were disinterred and sent to their hometowns at the request of their respective families. Moore started a fence around the graveyard using boards that his workers found inside and outside of the stockade. On August 17, 1865, his troops raised the first United States flag at the site of an infamous prison camp that reportedly had never had a Confederate flag. Lieutenant C.E. Moore, and then Captain A.W. Corliss, finished the work. Corliss employed from some fifty to two hundred workers under the supervision of a corporal and six soldiers.

A postwar engraving of the cemetery at Andersonville. Today, Andersonville is the only combined national historic site and cemetery. *Courtesy of the Library of Congress.*

These improvements persuaded the War Department not to remove the bodies to somewhere more accessible to visitors. Congress made the graves of the Andersonville dead a national cemetery, with a permanent, paid government superintendent, on November 11, 1865. The bodies would remain where prisoners—and, after too many members of the burial details escaped, slaves—buried them in 1864–65, usually without coffins or other amenities.

By 1868, 868 other Union soldiers had also received relocation to the Andersonville cemetery from Americus, Columbus, Eufaula, Macon and elsewhere. The Andersonville survivors who later died at Camp Lawton in Millen, Georgia, however, where reburied at the national cemetery in Beaufort, South Carolina, in 1869, as if returning them to Andersonville might have been an indignity.

For many years, the Women's Relief Corps, founded in 1869 under the local leadership of Elizabeth Ann Thompson, made the greatest effort at maintaining the cemetery. In 1877, tombstones of Georgia marble replaced the wooden grave markers, although some private individuals also provided tombstones for soldiers close to them. The Women's Relief Corps erected a fence around the graves in 1878.

Andersonville National Cemetery, circa 1910. *Courtesy of Georgia Archives, Vanishing Georgia Collection, Sum101.*

This historic ground at Anderson Station drew tourists from its very beginnings, including Southern women, who were allowed to climb into the guard towers to see often near-naked captive Yankees. Some of the women threw food into the giant pen, but others jeered. The curious, family and friends traveled after the war to see the graves and ruins of Camp Sumter at Anderson Station. In the first year after the war, Andersonville reportedly drew some ten thousand visitors, undoubtedly making it war-torn Georgia's sole tourist attraction. Various state monuments to the dead would be erected in the cemetery and near the stockade site in later years. The dedications would cause surges in visitations. Visitors would collect souvenirs from the prison grounds, some of which would later be displayed on tours across the country with the result of spreading the infamy of the camp even more.

For the survivors of the prison, their return as visitors could be emotionally overwhelming, as reported to the press:

These men, whatever their natural temper, the superintendent says, can almost be distinguished by the effects of fear, dread, and vivid recollection which come back like a shock into their faces as they again stand on the now quiet and sunlit scene of their experiences.

Above: Anderson station after the war. *Courtesy of the Andersonville National Historic Site and Peggy Sheppard.*

Right: Veterans assemble around one of the sites that they remembered as the Providence Spring, which provided them with desperately needed drinking water in the summer of 1864. Fewer than one thousand of the almost forty thousand men who entered Andersonville Prison were said to still be alive by 1890. *Courtesy of the Andersonville National Historic Site.*

Most of two completed stockade walls still stood as late as 1873. Ten years later, only one wall remained. In 1888, only one pole of the wall still stood. All of the prison buildings had disappeared by then, although the stumps of the rotted palisades still indicated the location of the walls. Holes that had once been the homes of the prisoners, some cannon barrels and the earthen walls of the forts remained. The open wells became a deathtrap for livestock. The swamp through the middle of the grounds and the Providence Spring disappeared.

The old soldiers argued endlessly in their veterans' newspapers about the location and circumstances of the lightning strike in August 1864 that allegedly led to the creation of the Providence Spring, a badly needed source for clean drinking water. In 1883, H.S. Beaman of Beaman, Iowa, paid to have what he remembered as the spring cleared out and then walled. Visitors would frequently picnic by its waters, as it became a fishpond that deer and other wild animals frequented. In 1901, the Women's Relief Corps

Memorial Day 1911 at the Iowa Monument, Andersonville. *Courtesy of Georgia Archives, Vanishing Georgia Collection, Sum151.*

of the Grand Army of the Republic erected a white marble springhouse over the Providence Spring, to which the National Association of Union Ex-Prisoners of War added a fountain dedicated to all of the Andersonville prisoners. In the 1880s, K.G. Kennedy, a former slave, owned and planted cotton on the site of the stockade.

The stockade had completely vanished by 1890, when a committee of the Commander E.S. Jones Post Number 5 of the Georgia Department of the Grand Army of the Republic visited the site. Captain I.D. Crawford, commander of that GAR post, and Dr. J.W. Stone of Atlanta bought most of the prison grounds on December 30, 1890, from freedman George W. Kennedy (the previously mentioned K.G. Kennedy?). Under public pressure, they abandoned their idea of making it into a moneymaking museum and reconstruction of the stockade. They finally offered to clear the last remains of the prison for a public park.

With the encouragement of Crawford, the Georgia Division of the Grand Army of the Republic, formed in 1889, almost immediately began efforts to acquire the site of the stockade to protect it from inappropriate use. The GAR had problems with raising funds and formally incorporating, however. Dr. Stone traveled to the North to find donations for the prison project. Crawford and Stone served on the Board of Control connected with the GAR to oversee clearing the brush and restoring parts of the prison. The board further planned to build a museum, supported in part by accommodations for visiting veterans. The Georgia GAR finally purchased the seventy-one acres that included most of the rest of the prison site on September 19, 1892, for $1,550. The GAR hired George W. Kennedy to mark the lines of the old stockade with posts and to build a cover over the Providence Spring. The National Cemetery superintendents, starting with J.W. Bryant, helped the GAR lease the grounds that lacked historical significance to farmers, including Kennedy.

Local people benefited little from the national interest in the old prison. Some nearby residents searched the site for treasure buried and lost by prisoners and guards. Many of their neighbors avoided the site, as they claimed that the ground was haunted with strange noises, flying swords and unexplained fires. As late as 1888, the community had only added a depot building to stand with the squalid three or four old houses. At that time, M.P. Suber, depot manager since the war, still held that position. This community missed the opportunity of developing into a substantial town when the Buena Vista Railroad bypassed it in 1886. Three years later, former POW Samuel

Entrance to the prison site in the early 1900s. *Courtesy of Georgia Archives, Vanishing Georgia Collection, Sum102.*

Creelman found that the newly incorporated town of Andersonville had only some eight or ten dwellings and a hotel. In the decades that followed, the countryside around Andersonville earned positive notoriety, encouraging local people to want to bury the prison's past. Charles Lindbergh bought his first airplane and made his solo flight near the prison site; bauxite and kaolin mining became a major industry; and Reverend Clarence Jordon started the international biracial farming cooperative of Koinonia in Americus. In 1976, nearby native son James Earl Carter became the thirty-ninth president of the United States and was later a recipient of the Nobel Peace Prize. His kinsmen included at least one Andersonville guard, Jesse Taliaferro Carter of the Third Georgia Reserves.

Local resentment of commemoration and popular remembrance of the prison's notoriety began on May 30, 1870. On that day, Georgia's widely despised Reconstruction governor Rufus Bullock gave a public address from a wagon at Andersonville, where, while reciting stories of the horrors of the prison camp, he claimed to have witnesses present to testify that six prisoners were taken out of the camp, tied up and then eaten alive by the camp's dog packs. General Phil Cook of Oglethorpe refused to tolerate this tirade. He mounted another wagon and challenged the governor to produce the witnesses. No one came forward.

Many Southerners opposed any commemoration of a Confederate-operated prison, even a century after the gates closed. Former slaves had begun conducting Memorial Day services at the cemetery after the war, and the Georgia Division GAR made the services a formal annual event, starting on May 30, 1889. The ceremony drew crowds of thousands of visitors, including hecklers from outside the Andersonville community. Some Georgians also resented the reunions held at Andersonville by Federal veterans groups, especially when the old soldiers became drunk and rowdy or when these gatherings involved African Americans and white men together. Troops from Fort McPherson began providing security.

In 1896–97, the GAR gave the prison site to the Women's Relief Corps (WRC). The WRC acquired an additional fourteen and a half acres of the prison site property from local landowners. The women also had the grounds

Demonstrations at Andersonville against memorializing the Civil War, 1975. *Courtesy of Georgia Archives, Vanishing Georgia Collection, Sum110.*

Girl Scouts placing flags at Andersonville National Cemetery, Memorial Day 1976. *Courtesy of Georgia Archives, Vanishing Georgia Collection, Sum119.*

cleared, bridges erected and a driveway graded. For the caretaker and visitors, the WRC erected a nine-room house, with a view of the grounds, on the north side of the stockade site.

A new storm of controversy about the prison began when the United Daughters of the Confederacy (UDC) planned to erect a monument to Captain Henry Wirz. Reaction to a memorial to Wirz proved so negative that the UDC failed to get permission for one, even in Atlanta. Macon, Richmond and Savannah wanted the memorial, but it finally went up in the town of Andersonville in 1909. Critics called it the only monument on American soil erected to brutality. Vandals desecrated it in 1919. In 1939, efforts to build a "peace monument" in the national cemetery that would unite North and South by presenting Southern excuses for Andersonville failed, and in 1958, the UDC could not obtain an appropriation from the Georgia legislature to have the Wirz monument repaired.

The modern history of the prison site began when the Women's Relief Corps turned control of the site over to the War Department under an act of

This page: The site of the prison stockade today. *Author's collection.*

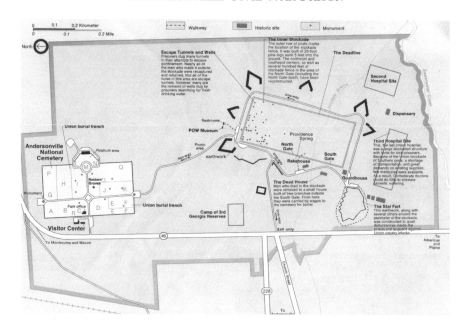

TURN YOU TO THE STRONGHOLD
YE PRISONERS OF HOPE
ZECHARIAH 9:12

Above: Andersonville National Historic Site and National Cemetery. *Courtesy of the National Park Service.*

Left: The Georgia Monument, Andersonville National Cemetery. *Author's collection.*

Congress on March 2, 1910. The Federal government and former prisoners had already marked the major sites in the stockade with signs and posts. On August 10, 1933, Andersonville Prison Park and other Federal Civil War sites came under the auspices of the Office of National Parks (returned to its earlier name of the National Park Service in 1934) in the Department of the Interior. At that time, the Depression-era Civilian Conservation Corps (CCC) filled in the postwar gullies and dug ditches to prevent further erosion. The CCC also replaced the wooden markers in the park with stone. Andersonville National Historic Site formally came into existence on July 1, 1970, and on the following October 16, the adjoining national cemetery also became part of the site. Today, Andersonville includes the site of the prison, the still-active national cemetery, a research library and, opened in 1998, the National Prisoner of War Museum.

Notoriety from Mackinlay Kantor's 1955 Pulitzer Prize–winning novel *Andersonville* did not encourage a serious scholarly history of the prison until Ovid L. Futch's 1968 *History of Andersonville Prison*, a work of solid scholarship that has only been followed by four other histories of the prison. Today, tens of thousands of people from around the world come to the park each year. Many of them descend from men once held there, including the victims who remain in the cemetery. Other visitors, including myself, have guards or members of the garrison as ancestors, and still others come just to see what remains of one of the world's most notorious places.

Bibliography

Blakey, Arch Frederic. *General John H. Winder, C.S.A.* Gainesville: University of Florida Press, 1990.

Boyd, Harry G. "Civil War Prisoners of War: A Study of the Changes in Disposition of Federal and Confederate Prisoners of War, Between the Shelling of Fort Sumter and the Surrender at Appomattox Courthouse." PhD diss. California State University, 1992.

Brown, Daniel P. *The Tragedy of Libby and Andersonville Prison Camps: A Study of Mismanagement and Inept Logistical Policies*. Ventura, CA: Golden West Historical Publications, 1980.

Brown, Louis A. *The Salisbury Prison: A Case Study of Confederate Military Prisons, 1861–1865*. Wendell, NC: Avera Press, 1980.

Bryant, William O. *Cahawba Prison and the* Sultana *Disaster*. Tuscaloosa: University of Alabama Press, 1990.

Cangemi, Joseph P., and Casimir J. Kowalski, eds. *Andersonville Prison: Lessons in Organizational Failure*. Lanham, MD: University Press of America, 1992.

Davis, Robert S. *Ghosts and Shadows of Andersonville: Essays on the Social Histories of America's Deadliest Prison*. Macon, GA: Mercer University Press, 2006. The research files and notes from this book have been donated to the Hargrett Rare Book and Manuscripts Library, University of Georgia Libraries.

Denny, Robert E. *Civil War Prisons & Escapes: A Day by Day Chronicle*. New York: Sterling Publishing, 1993.

Futch, Ovid L. *History of Andersonville Prison*. Gainesville: University of Florida Press, 1968.

Gardner, Douglas Gibson. "Andersonville and American Memory: Civil War Prisoners and Narratives of Suffering and Redemption." PhD diss. Miami University, 1998.

Gillispie, James M. *Andersonvilles of the North: The Myths and Realities of Northern Treatment of Civil War Confederate Prisoners*. Denton: University of North Texas Press, 2008.

Hesseltine, William B. *Civil War Prisons: A Study in War Psychology*. New York: Frederick Ungar, 1964.

Koerting, Gayla M. "The Trial of Henry Wirz and Nineteenth Century Military Law." PhD diss. Kent State University, 1995.

Lynn, John W. *800 Paces to Hell: Andersonville*. Fredericksburg, VA: Sergeant Kirkland's Museum, 1999.

Marvel, William. *Andersonville: The Last Depot*. Chapel Hill: University of North Carolina Press, 1994.

Roberts, Edward F. *Andersonville Journey*. Shippensburg, VA: Burd Street Press, 1998.

Ruhlman, R. Fred. *Captain Henry Wirz and Andersonville Prison*. Knoxville: University of Tennessee Press, 2006.

Segars, J.H. *Andersonville: The Southern Perspective*. Atlanta, GA: Southern Heritage Press, 1995.

Sheppard, Peggy. *Andersonville Georgia U.S.A.* Leslie, GA: Sheppard Publications, 1973.

Sneden, Robert Knox. *Eye of the Storm: A Civil War Odyssey*. New York: Free Press, 2000.

———. *Images from the Storm*. New York: Free Press, 2001.

Speer, Lonnie R. *Portals to Hell: Military Prisons of the Civil War*. Mechanicsburg, PA: Stackpole Books,1997.

INDEX

K

Kantor, Mackinlay 39, 94, 133
Karnes, Emily 69
Keen, Joseph 89
Kellogg, Robert H. 46, 56, 82, 88
Kennedy, George W. 127
Kennedy, K.G. 127
Key, Leroy L. 82, 96, 100
Kiene, Peter 40
Kirby, John F. 43
Koinonia, GA 128

L

Larkin, Goody 99
LeBron, Lawrence 30, 75, 88
Leonard, Isaac Newton 41
Leonard, Margaret Larney 41
Levitt, Saul 117
Libby Confederate Prison
     (Richmond, VA) 9, 16, 17
Limber Jim 92, 93, 94, 95, 96, 97,
     99, 100, 101
Lindbergh, Charles 128
Lugenbeal, William 35
Lundquist, Jack 5, 33, 38

M

Macon (city), Bibb County, GA 9,
     21, 26, 27, 30, 31, 32, 43, 44,
     51, 54, 60, 61, 68, 79, 80, 81,
     82, 83, 85, 104, 105, 109,
     110, 111, 121, 123, 130
Macon County, GA 9, 21, 79, 121
Maddox, Frank 73
Maddox, Robert F. 27
Mallory, Jim 82
Manigault, Louis 58
Marvel, William 26, 38, 94, 114
Mason, Thomas D. 86
Mattock, Frank. See Maddox, Frank
Maxson, Joseph C. 99

McCullough, Pete 97
McElroy, John 56, 70, 74, 89
McGinley, J.S. 25
McLaughlin or McGlaughlin,
     James 100
McNealy, J.M. 25
Melville, Herman 93
Memorial Day services 129
Methodist church in Andersonville
     25
Milledgeville, GA 88, 105
Millen, GA 10, 14, 31, 68, 107,
     123
Moore, C.E. 122
Moore, James M. 122
Moore, Sidney 73
Morris, John H. 94
mortality rate 12
Muir, Andrew. See Munn, Andrew
Munn, Andrew 99

N

National Association of Union Ex-
     Prisoners of War 127
National Prisoner of War Museum
     133
Native Americans 55
Near Andersonville 78
Newby, William 62, 63
Noirto, Sylvester 109
North Carolinians at Andersonville
     56
Northrop, John 56, 71
Northrop, John W. 56

O

O'Connell, Bartholomew 84
Olinger, Henry E. 99
Olustee, FL, Battle of 27, 33, 34
O'Neal, Edward 59
O'Neil, J.G. 35

ABOUT THE AUTHOR

R obert Scott Davis is the director of the Genealogy Program of Wallace State Community College, Hanceville, Alabama. His duties include helping to build one of the South's most extensive genealogical collections, operating a microfilming facility, teaching genealogy in one of the first colleges to offer genealogy as a college-level course and organizing field trips for his classes to libraries throughout the country. In 2006, his program received the Award for Outstanding Leadership in History from the American Association for State and Local History. Professor Davis also teaches survey courses in geography and history. He has more than one thousand publications of all sorts and from research he has conducted in archives and libraries throughout the United States, England and Scotland. His book *Ghosts and Shadows of Andersonville* is one of the first annalistic-style social histories of the American Civil War. Aside from writing history, genealogy and records, he has also compiled books and articles on methods and materials in research.

The author at the Henry Wirz Monument, Andersonville, Georgia. *Author's collection.*

Visit us at
www.historypress.net